CRAFT BREWERIES AND CITIES

This book brings together a diverse collection of case studies, perspectives, and research to explore how craft breweries have interacted with cities and neighborhoods in meaningful ways.

It provides a deeper understanding of the important issues facing neighborhoods, city government, and breweries, such as economic development, race and equity, crime, and sustainability. It demonstrates how craft breweries are meaningful contributors and participants in addressing these critical challenges. Written in an accessible style, this book contains contributions from a diverse array of research and professional backgrounds and personal perspectives. It allows readers to increase the dialogue across disciplines and build an evidence base regarding the interaction between communities and craft breweries.

This book appeals to undergraduate and graduate students as well as policy makers and industry professionals, working in urban studies, planning, public policy, business administration, economic development, and the craft brewery industry.

Julie Wartell is Continuing Lecturer in the Department of Urban Studies and Planning at the University of California, San Diego, and an independent advisor to governmental agencies and communities relating to analyzing crime problems, neighborhood safety, and the geography and economics of breweries. Julie currently teaches "GIS for Urban and Community Planning," "Craft Breweries and the Urban Economy," "Crime Prevention through Environmental Design," and "Crime Analysis Research Methods," and her research, training, and writing have been used in communities around the world. Julie has a master's degree in public administration from San Diego State University as well as a postgraduate diploma in applied criminology and police management from the University of Cambridge. In her spare time, Julie also runs PubQuest, a brewery mapping company.

Vince Vasquez is the executive director of the Policycraft Institute, an independent economic and public policy think tank based in Carlsbad, California. Vince has more than 18 years of experience in public policy research and analysis and has authored six studies on the craft brewing industry in San Diego County. Vince specializes in state and regional economic and workforce research, political analysis, and geographic information systems. Currently, Vince serves as the Director of Government Relations for National University, a non-profit, veteran-founded university based in San Diego, California, and has been affiliated with the University since 2009. Vince has a bachelor's degree in political science from the University of California, San Diego, and a master's degree in business administration from National University.

Routledge Critical Beverage Studies
Series edited by Peter J. Howland, Jennifer Smith Maguire
and Catherine May Tucker

Routledge Critical Beverage Studies offers cutting edge and ground-breaking
insights on beverages as vehicles for a wide array of social, cultural, economic,
environment and political phenomenon. Books in the series are interdisciplinary
and multi-methodological, exploring a variety of perspectives from the social
sciences and humanities.

The Wine & The Gift
From Production to Consumption
Edited by Peter J. Howland

Producing and Consuming the Craft Beer Movement
Wesley Shumar and Tyson Mitman

Craft Breweries & Cities
Perspectives from the Field
Edited by Julie Wartell and Vince Vasquez

For more information about this series, please visit: www.routledge.com/Routledge-
Critical-Beverage-Studies/book-series/CBS

Craft Breweries and Cities

Perspectives from the Field

**Edited by Julie Wartell
and Vince Vasquez**

Routledge
Taylor & Francis Group

LONDON AND NEW YORK

First published 2023
by Routledge
4 Park Square, Milton Park, Abingdon, Oxon OX14 4RN

and by Routledge
605 Third Avenue, New York, NY 10158

Routledge is an imprint of the Taylor & Francis Group, an informa business

British Library Cataloguing-in-Publication Data
A catalogue record for this book is available from the British Library

ISBN: 978-1-032-44314-0 (hbk)
ISBN: 978-1-032-44315-7 (pbk)
ISBN: 978-1-003-37156-4 (ebk)

DOI: 10.4324/9781003371564

Typeset in Times New Roman
by Apex CoVantage, LLC

This book is dedicated to the craft brewing industry of the past, current, and future as well as all of the government officials, businesses, and community that have helped the industry thrive. Cheers!

Contents

Figures

Tables

Contributors

Anna Domaradzka is a sociologist and an assistant professor and director at the Robert Zajonc Institute for Social Studies, University of Warsaw. She leads the Civil City Lab, an interdisciplinary research team focused on co-creation of better, more democratic, and wisely managed cities. Her research examines urban cohesion and mobilization, civil society, and social entrepreneurship as well as gender and social equality. Her particular interest is in how urban planning and technology can influence the implementation of the principles of democracy, equality, and social justice expressed by the "right to the city" concept. She's a board member of the International Society of Third Sector Research and ISA Research Committee 48 on Social Movements, Collective Action, and Social Change.

Russ Gibbon is the founder and current president of Blue Dome Consultants LLC, a small consulting firm specializing in industrial development. Mr. Gibbon formerly worked at the City of San Diego in its Economic Development Division for 26 years, during which time he facilitated over $3 billion worth of industrial development to create tax revenue for the city and job opportunities for its residents. Mr. Gibbon worked directly with business executives, developers, brokers, architects, engineers, and consultants throughout the city on hundreds of manufacturing, R&D, and distribution projects, from microbrewery projects up through Fortune 100 businesses. Mr. Gibbon was particularly instrumental in growing the local San Diego beer industry, having provided regulatory relief and direct support to all of the larger brewing companies in the city of San Diego.

Kevin Ham is the retired director of Economic Development for the City of Vista, California. In this role, he created one of the nation's largest craft brew clusters by identifying this emerging industry and working with them to grow and expand. Kevin led the revitalization of a historic downtown, taking it from an inactive environment to one that has become the community's active heart and soul. He was the key architect of a five-city economic development initiative called Innovate 78, which involved a cohesive brand strategy/marketing plan and an annual program of work.

Additionally, Kevin negotiated the sale, purchase, and lease of multiple properties that led to beneficial structural changes for the community, which doubled the size of a 7 million square foot industrial park. Kevin also spearheaded the development, adoption, and implementation of two city economic development strategic plans and served as an ombudsman for city businesses.

T. Dustin Hauck began his architectural career in 1996 and founded Hauck Architecture 12 years later. Prior to founding his own architecture firm, Mr. Hauck's early projects included high-end custom single-family homes, automotive repair/maintenance centers, and large hospitality projects. A member of the award-winning QUAFF home brew club since 2003, Dustin has a passion for the craft brewing industry. This allowed for an opportunity to design his first brewery project in 2012. Hauck Architecture has now been involved in over 200 brewery projects across the United States as well as coffee roasteries, distilleries, wineries, and craft beer–centric bars and restaurants, setting him apart as the premier brewery architect in the industry.

Greg Koch is the co-founder of Stone Brewing and Stone Distributing Co. He's done other things too, like building and operating the world's largest music rehearsal studio complex and real estate stuff and traveling to nearly 60 countries so far, but honestly nothing that anyone's paid any particular attention to save for the brewery part (and he suspects that folks will likely soon forget his role in that, and that's perfectly fine).

Joseph LeRoy is an Operations Coordinator and Adjunct Professor at DePaul University. He has a B.S. in Biological Sciences from the University of Tennessee and an MBA from DePaul University. He teaches on a broad variety of topics, though beer has always been his academic passion. When he's not engaged with university business, he can be found enjoying live music, attending beer festivals, and spending time with his friends and family. Always prepared with a recommendation for a local brewery, he's forever on the hunt for a new beer to sample. He is a father and husband, making his home in Chicago, IL.

Josh Newton is an urban planning and public policy PhD candidate in the College of Architecture, Planning, and Public Affairs at the University of Texas at Arlington and a Crossing Latinidades Mellon Fellow. His dissertation examines comprehensive community initiatives (CCIs). He is also working on research on the use of community development strategies by craft breweries, forms of precarity and grassroots adaptation in informal communities in the Dallas-Fort Worth Metroplex, philanthropic place-based interventions for social and environmental justice, and environmental justice in city council agenda setting. Josh teaches courses on race/ethnicity in US cities, the history of US urban communities, and urban design and planning theory.

Omar Passons is a former land use attorney and workforce and economic development professional and a longtime advocate for neighborhood issues impacting diverse communities. He is also a lover of independent craft beer and has organized celebrations of San Diego craft beer. Passons is an executive in local government, has served on the San Diego Workforce Development Board and the Management Committee of the Urban Land Institute, and has been a volunteer contributor to inclusive economic efforts across California. He received his undergraduate and Master of Public Health degrees at the University of Arizona and his law degree from George Mason University School of Law. He is a civic leader on issues impacting economic equity, homelessness, and creating opportunities for all members of the community to lead lives of dignity.

Neil Reid is a professor of geography and planning at the University of Toledo. Since 2014, Neil's research has focused on the social and economic impact that craft breweries have on their surrounding neighborhoods. This research has examined the impact of craft breweries on real estate prices, crime, and neighborhood revitalization. His research has also examined craft breweries as Third Places (neighborhood hangouts). Neil teaches a course on the Geography of Beer and Brewing at the University of Toledo and writes a beer blog (www.thebeerprofessor.com). He has also written pieces on the brewing industry for the *Wall Street Journal*, National Public Radio, and Salon.com.

Steve Shapiro has written about beer since 2007, when he co-founded the regional beer travel reference site BeerByBart.com, with Gail Ann Williams. He was an editor at Celebrator Beer News from 2009 to 2018. Their collaborative journalistic efforts on their own site and for a wide array of consumer craft beer journals have resulted in multiple reporting awards from the North American Guild of Beer Writers. In addition, Shapiro has traveled at the behest of local chambers and tourism organizations for the purpose of covering beer events. Shapiro places a personal priority on experiencing beer tourism, traveling to meet and interview beer people in their local communities, and exploring fresh beers from the source.

Vince Vasquez is the executive director of the Policycraft Institute, an independent economic and public policy think tank based in Carlsbad, California. Vince has more than 18 years of experience in public policy research and analysis and has authored six studies on the craft brewing industry in San Diego County. Vince specializes in state and regional economic and workforce research, political analysis, and geographic information systems. Currently, Vince serves as the Director of Government Relations for National University, a non-profit, veteran-founded university based in San Diego, California, and has been affiliated with the University since 2009. Vince has a bachelor's degree in political science from the University of

California, San Diego, and a master's degree in business administration from National University.

Julie Wartell is Continuing Lecturer in the Department of Urban Studies and Planning at the University of California, San Diego, and an independent advisor to governmental agencies and communities relating to analyzing crime problems, neighborhood safety, and the geography and economics of breweries. Julie currently teaches "GIS for Urban and Community Planning," "Craft Breweries and the Urban Economy," "Crime Prevention through Environmental Design," and "Crime Analysis Research Methods," and her research, training, and writing have been used in communities around the world. Julie has a master's degree in public administration from San Diego State University as well as a postgraduate diploma in applied criminology and police management from the University of Cambridge. In her spare time, Julie also runs PubQuest, a brewery mapping company.

Bartholomew Watson is Chief Economist at the Brewers Association – the national not-for-profit trade association for America's small and independent craft brewers – a role he has held since 2013. He leads the association's statistical, economic, and research efforts. Prior to that role, he was a visiting assistant professor at the University of Iowa, a lecturer at the University of California Berkeley, and an associate for the Barthwell Group, a management consulting firm. He holds a PhD from the University of California Berkeley.

Gail Ann Williams is a journalist with a focus on craft beer. She and Steve Shapiro have co-authored pieces for beer publications including CraftBeer.com, Celebrator Beer News, BeerAdvocate Magazine, The Alcohol Professor, Beer Paper LA, and other outlets, garnering several reporting awards from the North American Guild of Beer Writers. In 2007, she and Shapiro partnered to launch their own site, BeerByBART.com, to help locals and visitors explore the San Francisco Bay Area beer scene via public transportation such as the Bay Area Rapid Transit (BART) system. Williams also serves the craft brewing community as a Beer Judge Certification Program beer judge, informing her understanding of the evolution of craft beer styles.

Preface

Craft brewing has been a growing industry for more than a decade. While craft breweries make the news for a wide variety of reasons, our goal in creating *Craft Breweries and Cities* is to illustrate how the craft brewing industry has helped to shape contemporary communities and urban issues. This cross-section of research, case studies, and examples of breweries and cities are valuable learning opportunities for both current and aspiring industry professionals, scholars, and municipal leaders and can help foster greater dialogue, opportunities, and understanding in communities across the country.

We see the importance of collecting, preserving, and sharing these unique experiences and stories that colleagues and other subject matter experts have had over the years, to share with future generations and other communities, especially those where the craft brewery industry is not included or incorporated into community dialogues or civic planning. There are few published resources available that aim to demonstrate how craft breweries are meaningful contributors and participants in addressing critical challenges that cities and urban communities are facing today.

Our authors come from a diverse array of research and professional backgrounds and personal perspectives. We cover issues ranging from overall demographic and geographic trends to community, economic, and workforce development to gentrification, land use, zoning, and regulations and from adaptive reuse to racial equity and sustainability, with chapters on crime and craft beer tourism. Across these twelve chapters, readers will learn how the power of ideas, ingenuity, creativity, and collaboration that is driving breweries and industry entrepreneurs is now being channeled toward greater civic causes in cities across the United States and beyond.

Because these issues about breweries' interactions with cities are topical and evolving, there are constant examples of these same subjects regularly in the news. There is a theme of "place" throughout the book, but one thing not mentioned is how breweries often associate with their neighborhoods and cities through the naming and labeling of their breweries and beers. While several chapters discuss municipalities changing zoning and regulations to encourage breweries, one of the earliest examples of this was in Delaware when the state began to allow brewpubs to accommodate the new Dogfish

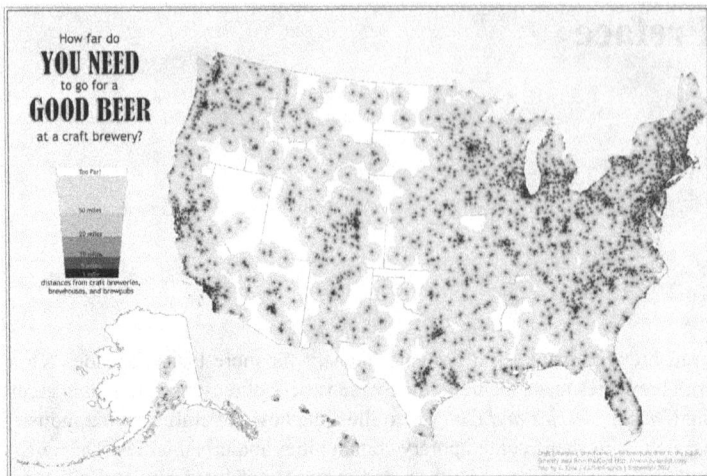

Figure 0.1 How far do you need to go for a good beer at a craft brewery?

Head Brewing.[1] We have one chapter focused solely on sustainability, but this is such a timely and important issue that new data, studies, and innovations are constantly arriving. The state of New Hampshire recently recognized a craft brewery as its first "Sustainable Craft Beverage."[2]

Some clarifying points as you read this book: Throughout the book, the term "breweries" is most used, but this includes multiple types of brewery establishments – tasting rooms with production, restaurants with production facilities attached, and tasting rooms/restaurants owned by breweries and serving their beer but with no brewing onsite. Local jurisdictions, state governments, and regulatory agencies may have varying definitions according to licensing and zoning as well.

We hope you enjoy learning about these important issues relating to breweries and cities. We've included a map of breweries across the United States to give readers the initial perspective of where the 9,000 breweries are located. Feel free to pop open a local #craftbeer while reading.

Julie Wartell and Vince Vasquez

San Diego 2023

Notes

1 More on this in the podcast about the founding of Dogfish Head – https://podcasts. apple.com/us/podcast/dogfish-head-craft-brewery-sam-and-mariah-calagione/ id1150510297
2 See www.des.nh.gov/news-and-media/throwback-brewery-recognized-new-hamp shires-first-sustainable-craft-beverage.

Foreword

Fifty years ago, when Jack McAuliffe established the New Albion Brewery in Sonoma, California, to make British pale ales, few would have predicted that idea would grow as it has. Today, there are nearly 10,000 craft breweries and brewpubs that command almost 27% of the US beer market. I was excited by Jack's ideas and had a close-up of his thinking.

Whether Jack knew that the movement New Albion represented would affect virtually every aspect of the brewing industry worldwide, I cannot tell, but that's the way it turned out. These days we cannot really think about, or talk about, or do anything in brewing, without taking into account that the craft industry exists and that its needs should be accommodated. The creative genius and rampant entrepreneurship of those who have built major brewing companies have not merely set the tone for the beer industry but have fostered similar inventiveness in many other aspects of the drinks world and even of some foods.

We might even say that craft beers have created a class of consumers ready to explore a much wider world of products and flavors than previously existed, and that has opened new opportunities for entrepreneurs to invent those products.

These ideas are far from new. These are ideas within the craft beer industry paying deserved homage to its own success. There are many books that examine these technical aspects of the industry, from the hard-core science and technology of the process itself, to supply chain management, to the nitty gritty of managing a complex business, among many others.

As far I can tell, there is no book quite like this one; it explores a new and different territory. This book examines in detail how a craft brewery or brewpub fits into or adds to or detracts from or serves or is affected by the community in which it is embedded. The fact that craft brewing businesses of several kinds are now so numerous and broadly distributed makes it possible to study the industry using established social science methods and to evaluate the results in appropriate related contexts. This book is not an examination of the industry so much as an exploration of its affect upon its environment or the effect of the environment on the industry.

There are many aspects to that, which, frankly, I had never thought of and have not previously seen pulled together in this way. Here many such ideas are explored: demographics and socio-economics of location, reusing old buildings and neighborhood revitalization, ale trails and craft beer tourism, gentrification and equity, community development, crime, workforce development and economic growth, city government relations and regulations reform, sustainability, zoning laws and restrictions, among many others. There are also two case studies.

Who should read this book? There are of course many professionals and students in such fields as urban and community development and socio-economics who should read this book, but I think also professional brewers need to have a good understanding of the impact or potential impact of their business on the community or of the community on their business. Knowing this local impact may be a means of superior community relations or making sure that a business will be welcomed as a community asset.

Michael J. Lewis
Professor Emeritus of Brewing Science
University of California-Davis

Acknowledgments

We would like to first acknowledge our valued contributors, who shared their time and expertise as part of this endeavor. Your diligence, passion, and commitment were critical to making this reader happen. We also would like to thank those that have been part of the reviewing, editing, and development phases of this reader – Sarah McTague, Erik Bruvold, David Barnett, and Elizabeth Groff. Thank you to Barbara Kent for the map contribution, and lastly, we are honored to have the foreword written by Michael Lewis, the first professor of brewing science in the Americas. We appreciate you all and your efforts.

Section I

Overview

1 Craft Brewery Geography and Demography Trends

A Primer

Bartholomew Watson

Introduction

Where is craft brewing industry growth and development headed, and what does that mean for our changing communities? The last two decades have seen exponential growth in the craft brewing industry in the United States, rising from 1,487 craft breweries in 2001 to 9,118 in 2021. While this growth has happened in all parts of the country, from small, rural towns to our largest cities and metropolitan areas, it has not been evenly distributed. This chapter will discuss these geographic patterns, including trends in brewery production and economic impact by area. We have also seen changes in the demographics of craft brewery owners, brewers, and consumers, which will be examined. In all, we will explore some of the patterns and contradictions that drive brewery location, both across and within cities, and how they interact with the geography of craft consumers.

A basic understanding of brewery location starts with a simple statement, which will gain more complexity over the course of this chapter: breweries are located where people live. To a certain extent, this has always been true. If you look at a map of current multinational brewery (Anheuser-Busch InBev and MolsonCoors) locations, or the location of breweries when that number hit its nadir in the late 1980s, they are distributed in such a way that those locations sit as close to major US population centers as possible. Beer is mostly water; water is heavy, and there is a lot of cost associated with moving heavy things over long distances.

Even as the brewery number has expanded exponentially, and the market has moved away from one where brewery numbers were determined by minimum efficient scale (see Tremblay et al., 2005) to one with a higher service component, breweries still have strong incentives to locate close to people. Taprooms and brewpubs rely on customer traffic for their business model, and so, larger population centers can support more brewery businesses. In 2021, the correlation between a state's 21+ population and the number of active breweries was 0.86 (analysis of Brewers Association data, 2022). Flipping around, more than 80% of Americans live within 10 miles of a brewery (Brewers Association, 2021; Patterson et al., 2022).

DOI: 10.4324/9781003371564-2

However, as we begin looking across states, within states, and within cities, those relationships begin to show huge variations, or even disappear. There is huge and persistent variation in the number of breweries across states (see Watson, 2020, June 25). Urban areas with more people have fewer breweries per capita than those with fewer people. These variations highlight the political and economic forces that drive large variations and even contradict the basic notion that where there are people, there are breweries (and vice versa). While this chapter won't consider environmental dimensions, the growing pressure on fresh water in certain locations is potentially another source of future variation that is worth exploring (see Chapter 8 on sustainability issues).

Another unexplored piece of brewery location is owner location and motivation. While there are certainly breweries that broadly choose locations based on extensive analysis, most owners are going to open a brewery relatively close to where they live. This is clearly one portion of the breweries-locate-where-there-are-people equation, since it is people who choose to locate breweries. Within those parameters, brewery owners must then consider a wide variety of other variables related to business viability, costs, and their own personal preferences. This chapter may have things to say about the first of those but will not explore the individual location preferences of owners, which could be an interesting area for future research.

Urban–Rural Brewery Location

First, let's examine the variations in urban versus rural brewery locations. This is a perfect area to test general questions about business viability and how breweries might choose to balance the lower market potential but lower costs that typically come with lower population densities. This isn't a simple linear relationship, and highly successful business models have been built around the notion that lower population densities might be preferable if a business is able to draw from a larger geographic area (one of the central insights in the Walmart business model). There may also be variations in planning and zoning and even regulatory advantages for urban versus rural breweries (as an example, farm brewery licenses might privilege rural breweries).

Looking closer, the Census Bureau's data was used on urbanized areas and clusters with a brewery data from 2018. Urbanized areas are regions of 50,000 people or more, and urban clusters run from 2,500 to 50,000 people. Anything else is considered outside an "urban" area – so this definition of rural will include small towns with less than 2,500 people that aren't associated with a larger urban area.

Rural breweries have increased overall but decreased as a percentage. The results are fascinating and show that as a percentage, the number of breweries in rural areas and the towns under 2,500 people has decreased as a percentage of all breweries between 2013 and 2018, despite a growth of 129%

in the number of those breweries overall (note that total brewery growth was 142% between 2013 and 2018).

For the 2018 data, a geographic information system (GIS) was used for the analysis. Although the results are very highly correlated, the GIS analysis found that a much higher percentage (15.6%) of breweries fall outside of Census-defined urban places. The difference is likely due to the higher sensitivity of the GIS analysis and that many breweries are just outside city limits but still within ZIP codes covered by those cities. Because limitations in the data mean a comparable 2013 GIS analysis cannot be done, the focus is on the ZIP code analysis. That said, there are often interesting research opportunities in this type of disconnect, and the possibility that breweries are choosing to locate on the edge of urban areas is another interesting area for future research.

Number of breweries per capita is inversely related to urban population. Compiling this data leads to a very interesting secondary finding – that the number of breweries per capita is actually inversely related to the urban population. So, here we have our first great contradiction – or perhaps modification – to the basic starting point that where there are people, there are breweries. Where there are people, there are breweries, but where those people are most densely clustered, there are relatively fewer breweries.

For the largest urban areas, this makes a great deal of sense. Not only are those places typically pretty expensive, but they are already going to have a very competitive landscape of food and beverage options. Currently, there are only 100 more breweries in the most populated urban areas (5M+) as there are in rural areas/the smallest towns.

Even more interesting is that the per capita numbers continue to increase as you go lower in population and that urban clusters with 2,500 to 10,000 people actually have the most breweries per capita. Those areas have 7.6% of the breweries in the country, despite only representing 3.5% of the US population (although their population may be larger if you included outlying rural areas that use those clusters for commercial services). One explanation for this finding could be a combination of lower costs, easier entry (via zoning/regulation), and lower competition. For some places, tourism might play a role, but it is not likely that a high percentage of towns that size are tourist destinations. Finally, as the difference between the GIS analysis and the ZIP analysis showed, it's possible that many small towns are "bigger" than their defined population and may actually draw on a bigger population base from outlying rural areas. All that said, there might be opportunities to explore preferences for local beer by urban area or other explanations by urban area size in future research.

State is Still a Better Predictor than Population. Analysis shows that these urban area population findings are much weaker than state effects. Although this analysis is a bit messy since some urban areas cut across state lines, knowing the state that a city is located in is a much better predictor of how many breweries per capita a city has than how many people it has (again, population of course matters for the total number of breweries). To summarize, as total number of breweries grew, both urban and rural breweries also increased but in different patterns by both urban area size and state.

These patterns might look different during this period of rapid growth than they will going forward in a more competitive environment when location effects might be larger determinants of business success. As the data shows, rural areas still have fewer breweries per capita but obviously far less density to draw on. It will also be interesting to watch the closing patterns in the future to see if one model proves more sustainable than another.

Demographics, Location, and the Demographics of Locations

Given that we have started to sketch out where breweries are located, the next topic might be how those locations line up with brewery customers. To do so, we are going to move down a level in geography to the Census tract level. In this section, we ask two major questions:

1. Who are craft brewery customers and how has that evolved over recent years?
2. How do the demographics of brewery locations compare both to their customers and to the general US population?

The data set used for this analysis looks at the presence and count of breweries (in mid-2020) by Census tract (determined using GIS) and then matches that count with demographic data on median household income, race/ethnicity, and age by gender for each tract using data from the American Community Survey (ACS). As a disclaimer – demographics are one of the social sciences where the data is the best and the causal inferences are the hardest. Because so many demographic variables are related, isolating one or two while missing another that might be confounding makes analysis challenging. In addition, demographics are not destiny, in that knowing someone's race/ethnicity/income/age may give you averages, but it tells you nothing about individual circumstances, and those same variables mean different things in different places with different cultural or political context. Hence, the "why" may be lacking at times.

Let's start with a high-level look at craft demographics, starting with gender. This data comes from Scarborough, a division of Nielsen, and covers a time period from August 2012 through November 2019.[1] This data uses a target of consumption of "any microbrew/craft beer" in the past 30 days. The number and demographics of craft drinkers do vary a lot depending on which frequency you use,[2] but this narrower approach finds that 8.4% of the

21+ population drinks craft regularly (past month), up from 6.6% in 2013 (and up from 7.4% and 7.3% in the 2014–15 and 2016–17 surveys).[3] In other words, the craft-drinking population continues to grow, 8.4% from 6.6%, which equals almost six million new drinkers. That's also roughly in line with the growth in craft production during that time period, approximately 40% (Brewers Association).

The time series of this data set also reveals positive signs in terms of better gender balance, with craft's gender percentage moving from 69.2% male and 30.8% female in 2013 to 65.9% male and 34.1% female in 2019. Note: we don't know much about entry/exit based on these types of surveys – meaning, is the additional 1.8% of the population from the same 6.6% and a new 1.8%, or is it, for example, a new 2.8% and loss of 1%? Even with the improved gender balance, there exists plenty of room for improvement. Because of the bigger base percentage for men, that change suggests 3.3 million new male craft drinkers against 2.5 million new female craft drinkers, so the incremental percentages are 57% male and 43% female.

Next, let's take a look at age demographics. One of the biggest long-term opportunities that I've seen for craft is that it might "hold" its demographic as craft drinkers age. Historically, beer has drawn a high proportion of its customer base from younger, legal-drinking-age consumers. As those consumers have aged, some of them have moved out of the beer category, partially due to lower volume consumption but more so because they "trade up" to what they see as more sophisticated or socially acceptable options, which previously had benefited wine. With the explosion of craft breweries, beer styles, and higher priced beers designed for a broader range of occasions beyond "refreshment," craft has had a chance to rewrite this narrative. There are beer options in fine-dining, and bringing a special bottle of beer or four-pack to the boss's holiday party is an option now. Does that mean that craft's demographic is aging? The data does suggest some positive signs.

Table 1.1 shows the index from 2013 and 2019. An index of 100 means that the percent of people in that income bracket is the same as the percent in

Table 1.1 Index of craft consumption by age, 2013 and 2019

Age Range	2013	2019
21–24	153	135
25–34	159	158
35–44	125	123
45–54	86	100
55–64	76	73
65+	36	37

Source: Nielsen Scarborough.

the total US population that drinks craft. If the national rate is 8%, that means 8% of that income bracket drinks craft. If the index is 50, that means the rate in that bracket is 50% of the national rate (so about 4%). And an index of 200 means that the rate for that bracket is two times the national rate (about 16%). Craft not only still over indexes those within the 35 to 44 age range, but that index has slightly increased. Similarly, it's improved its index those aged 45 to 54 years (people who were largely 35–44 in 2013) up to 100, meaning that age demographic has the same ratio of craft drinkers as the overall population. At the same time, the mean and median age did not move that much, with the mean increasing from 41.6 to 42.4 from 2013 to 2019, and the median moving from 39.7 to 39.8. And since the country has "aged" since 2013, some of that is just the shift toward an older US population in general.

Next, let's look at income. Table 1.2 is a table of craft drinkers for various household income brackets. It uses the same indices described earlier, where 100 means that the percent of people in that income bracket is the same as the percent in the total US population that drinks craft.

What the overall indices show is that craft skews toward higher income, and the time series shows that this has not changed much and, if anything, may have gotten more skewed over time; though with inflation, these income brackets are not completely comparable.

We see similar patterns when we look at the race/ethnicity data in Table 1.3. The only non-white category that has significantly improved its index from

Table 1.2 Index of craft consumption by income, 2013 and 2019

Household Income	2013	2019
Less than $35,000	47	38
$35,000–$49,999	67	54
$50,000–$74,999	111	96
$75,000–$99,999	132	118
$100,000–$249,999	177	176

Source: Nielsen Scarborough.

Table 1.3 Index of craft consumption by race and income, 2013 and 2019

Household Income	2013	2019
White	118	117
Black/African American	36	36
Asian	123	125
Hispanic/Latino	57	68
Other	104	96

Source: Nielsen Scarborough.

Table 1.4 Index of craft consumption by race and income, 2019

Household Income	White	Black	Hispanic
Less than $35,000	44	15	29
$35,000–$49,999	56	34	57
$50,000–$74,999	102	34	96
$75,000–$99,999	125	49	91
$100,000–$149,999	168	92	109
$150,000+	212	90	212

Source: Nielsen Scarborough.

2013 to 2019 is Hispanic, and Black/African-American continues to severely under-index.

Race and income are highly related in the United States; we can also look at this data in terms of race *and* income for various racial and ethnic groups for each year to try to separate these effects. What the data shows is that each racial and ethnic group has similar gaps in craft consumption between the highest and lowest income brackets. Table 1.4 shows 2019 data.

Income tells you part of the story, but even as income rises, Black/African-American and to a lesser extent Hispanic Americans don't consume craft at the same percentage rates as White Americans. A Black person in a household making more than $150,000 is actually less likely to consume craft than a White or Hispanic person in a household making $50,000–$74,999.

This is a quantification of both the opportunity and the hard work that craft brewers have in front of them if they wish to diversify their customer base. Putting aside systemic differences in income levels by race/ethnicity, if the craft category could simply achieve parity within income brackets, there would be millions of additional craft drinkers. Craft brewers can only play a partial role in larger systemic change, but they can choose to play a much bigger role in shrinking this gap.

Demographics of Brewery Locations

This challenge and opportunity are both going to overlap highly with location. Consequently, we can now turn to the demographics of where breweries are located by Census tract and how those locations match, or don't, the story told earlier, as well as the general patterns of US demographics.

Income

Based on the indices of craft consumption by income brackets, you might expect that craft brewers would be more likely to locate in higher income neighborhoods. That is not the case. Figure 1.1 shows breweries per 100,000 people

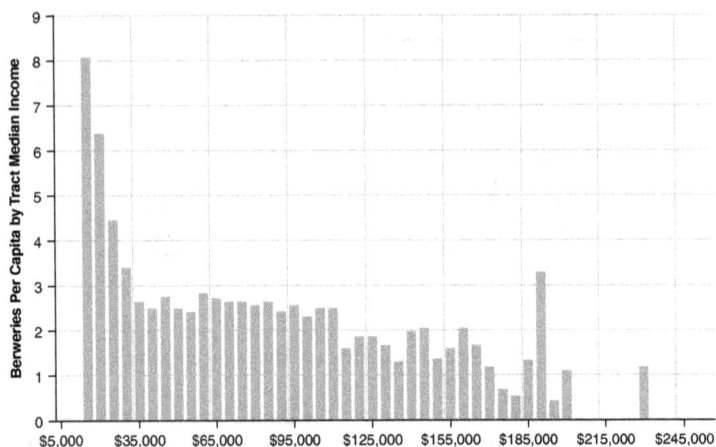

Figure 1.1 Breweries per 100,000 people for Census tracts across various incomes (brewery data from mid-2020).

for Census tracts across various incomes (brewery data from mid-2020). The highest breweries per capita occur in relatively low-income neighborhoods.

Presenting this data in per capita terms exaggerates this effect, even though these neighborhoods also have the highest number of breweries per tract if you cut it that way. In this data set, there are 2,803 census tracts with a median household income of $10,000–$25,000 (3.9% of the tracts that have an income estimate), and they have 5.8% of the breweries in the country. This gets even more exaggerated in per capita terms, since these areas only have 2.8% of the US population. Putting those data points together, you may quickly figure that these are relatively low population neighborhoods, suggesting they are industrial and warehouse districts with relatively low residential populations.

As you move up the income bracket, there are far more breweries (either per capita or per tract) in neighborhoods with incomes from $30,000 to $99,999 than there are in neighborhoods with incomes of $100,000+. The majority of breweries in the country are located in Census tracts with household incomes less than $60,000. In one sense, that's in line with national demographics: the median household income of Census tracts in this data set was $57,097, and the median for a tract with a brewery was $57,432 (it's a bit above it now, but this data set covers 2014–2018). However, as we just saw, craft drinkers skew much higher than the total US population. In 2017, the median household income of a craft drinker was closer to $90,000. In other words, breweries are located in neighborhoods that generally have incomes that are lower than the customer base of most breweries.

To sum, there is a clear gap between the income of neighborhoods where breweries are located and the income of their typical customers. This may be a logical business decision, as neighborhoods with lower median income may be located relatively close to higher income neighborhoods and offer lower rent or better zoning opportunities. Many breweries require space that is zoned for manufacturing, or simply space in general, so locating in residential neighborhoods may not be an option due to cost or space restrictions.[4]

Race/Ethnicity

Next, we look at the racial and ethnic makeup of brewery neighborhoods. On the surface, brewery and non-brewery tracts look pretty similar. Spatial analysis found an average population of 4,775 in brewery tracts versus 4,513 in non-brewery tracts, with an average size of 50.6 square miles for brewery tracts versus 49.3 for non-brewery tracts. The ACS data showed even closer average populations of 4,444 for brewery tracts and 4,438 for non-brewery tracts, which are essentially identical.

In terms of total population and size, on aggregate, brewery tracts and non-brewery tracts are not clearly different, and so, at the broadest possible level, clear confounds do not exist (it is likely that more would emerge with a deeper analysis). When we move to the race/ethnicity composition of tracts with a brewery versus those without, we begin to see clearer differences (see Table 1.5).

In short, the tracts with a brewery are in general whiter than those without a brewery. It is very hard to draw causality from these kinds of numbers and

Table 1.5 Race composition of tracts with no breweries, at least 1 brewery, clusters of breweries, and the most recent 2,000 breweries

	White	Black or African American	American Indian and Alaska Native	Asian	Native Hawaiian or Other Pacific Islander	Other Race alone or in combination with one or more other races	Hispanic or Latino, Total
No Breweries	60.2%	12.6%	0.7%	5.7%	0.2%	2.6%	18.3%
1 or more Breweries	70.8%	7.9%	0.7%	4.4%	0.1%	2.7%	13.4%
Brewery Clusters	61.1%	12.2%	0.7%	5.4%	0.2%	2.6%	17.8%
Most Recent 2,000	70.1%	8.8%	0.7%	4.0%	0.1%	2.6%	13.7%

Note: Percentages for "White," "Black or African American," etc. are for "non-Hispanic or Latino."

raises several questions. Are breweries locating in neighborhoods that look like what they think their core demographic will be? Is their location choice shaping those demographics? Is this more related to customer income and costs than it is to race or ethnicity? The last seems somewhat unlikely as a primary variable given what we just saw about household income in brewery Census tracts. Nevertheless, the answer is probably a bit of all of these and that those effects feed on each other.

This was further analyzed in two ways. First, looking at tracts with the highest brewery density. There are only 66 tracts that have 5 or more breweries, but those 66 tracts account for 425 breweries, or more than 5% of total US breweries. Second, looking at the most recent 2,000 breweries, which cover 1,841 different neighborhoods. Interestingly, for the brewery clusters (the 66 neighborhoods with the highest density of breweries), their racial/ethnic makeup is very similar to the total US population. It's not clear whether the makeup of those neighborhoods contributes to the brewery density or if there are other characteristics (cost/urban centers, etc.) that lead to them being ideal brewery locations. Whatever the drivers, these locations with clusters of breweries tend to look more like the total United States than they look like the demographics of craft beer drinkers.

In contrast, for the composition of the most recent 2,000 breweries, the racial/ethnic makeup of these locations are similar to where all US breweries are located. In other words, most breweries are going into places that already match up with the typical brewery location, although not the same neighborhoods. Of the 1,841 neighborhoods where the most recent 2,000 breweries are located, only 520 (28%) have another brewery in them. Meaning that most new breweries (72%) had 60,000+ neighborhoods to choose from (functionally less with zoning, etc.) but still picked neighborhoods with demographic patterns that look like where earlier breweries were located. This is a contributing factor in why the customer demographics in part one of this analysis have not changed much. For breweries to grow their demographic, they have to start doing new things – and while many individual breweries are, at least based on location relative to demographics, collectively new breweries are making basically the same geographic choices as the 6,000+ breweries that came before them.

The aforementioned data represents central tendency and, as such, also misses variation in the story. Figure 1.2 shows the frequency distribution of non-White population for tracts with and without a brewery. At nearly every percentage, there are breweries, but in the aggregate, you can clearly see that these distributions are not the same.

This distribution adds complexity to the story, perhaps partially overlapping with the income data described earlier. That said, this is the type of area that deserves longer investigation and analysis rather than speculation. For example, the location of breweries in areas that do not match national demographics does not necessarily speak to whether the demographics of those breweries themselves match their locations.

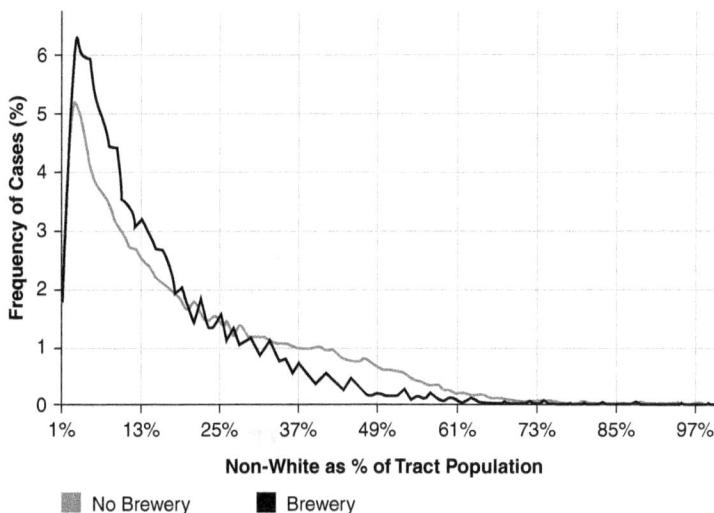

Figure 1.2 Frequency distribution of non-White population for tracts with and without a brewery.

Age is the simplest analysis. Neighborhoods with breweries have very similar age distributions to the total United States, to tracts without breweries, and to the most recent 2,000 brewery locations. The only part of the analysis that differs significantly is for the brewery cluster tracts containing 5 or more breweries. Those skew much younger than the US population, again suggesting central urban neighborhoods. Across the United States, age 21–44 equals about 44% of the 21+ population, and 45+ equals about 56%. In the brewery clusters, those percentages are flipped, with 58% from 21 to 44 and only 42% aged 45+.

Conclusion

This chapter started with a simple premise: breweries tend to be located where there are people. This makes sense, as it is people who both start breweries and are the customers (not to mention that beer is heavy, so moving it over far distances for people to drink doesn't make a lot of economic sense).[5] However, as we moved through urban versus rural, then demographics, and finally the demographics of specific brewery locations, we found complexity and nuance in this basic story. This is without introducing political and regulatory variables, which have long been shown to have strong effects on brewery location.[6]

While breweries locate where there are people, they tend to locate at higher rates in cities and towns with fewer people. They also don't necessarily locate in the precise places where their customers live, whether sliced by income or race/ethnicity. These decisions may be highly logical when viewed from a business perspective, accounting for zoning, space, cost factors, and clustering effects (see Nilsson et al., 2019 on brewery clusters or Porter, 1998 more generally on clusters). Nevertheless, they complicate and add questions to the narrative about brewery location.

Future research looking more specifically at a brewery level and understanding brewery customer demographics relative to where they are located would help build on these findings. Small and local breweries have long sold themselves partially by values extending beyond the beer, with community being one dimension. A greater understanding of when and how breweries engage with and represent the neighborhoods where they are located could help clarify when this story is true versus simply marketing.

Notes

1 The Scarborough data has huge sample sizes: 200,000 people in total. This allows reasonably large sample sizes even for niche markets like craft beer. For craft drinker demographics, samples are naturally smaller (since not everyone drinks craft), but the sample size ranges from 11,360 (2012–2013) to 18,551 (2018–2019).
2 www.brewersassociation.org/insights/shifting-demographics-among-craft-drinkers/
3 There is interesting variation in the demographics of craft drinkers based on what frequency is chosen. For the analysis that follows, using a less frequent definition of craft consumption as the base does show some evidence that female consumers have grown even more as a percentage of total craft drinkers. So women are trying craft at great rates (or drinking infrequently) but not always moving into more frequent consumption patterns.
4 See Chapters 5, 12, and 2 for additional research on neighborhood gentrification, zoning, and location characteristics.
5 The exception to this would be imported beer that because of the location or quality can be sold at enough of a premium to justify shipping costs. Even these cases tend to prove the rule. Mexican imports, the largest import category in the US, are largely produced on the border to minimize transport costs. Other successful imports in the US have often been on-shored in recent years for similar economic reasons.
6 See Burgdorf (2016) or Watson (2020). Other explanations include homebrewing legalization (McCullough et al., 2018).

Section II

Neighborhoods and the Urban Economy

2 Craft Breweries as Neighborhood Assets

Adaptive Reuse, Neighborhood Revitalization, and Third Places

Neil Reid

Introduction

In recent decades, craft breweries have emerged as a ubiquitous feature of the urban fabric of towns and cities in North America. In 2021, the United States and Canada were home to over 9,000 and 1,000 craft breweries respectively (Brewers Association, 2022; Canadian Craft Brewers Association, 2023). By volume, craft beer accounts for 13.1% of all beer sold in the United States, while in dollar terms it represents 26.7% of sales (Brewers Association, 2022). Attaining reliable market share data for craft breweries in Canada is challenging. However, one estimate suggests that craft beer accounts for approximately 10% of Canadian beer sales (Kirby & Lundy, 2022).

The growing number of craft breweries has attracted the attention of scholars in several disciplines, including economics, geography, and urban planning, who seek to understand their emergence from a variety of perspectives. Governmental officials, responsible for community and economic development have become increasingly interested in their growing popularity. They view craft breweries as enhancing neighborhood vibrancy and, in some cases, playing a catalytic role in re-energizing struggling neighborhoods (see for example Alexander, 2013; Hughes, 2018). In this chapter, drawing upon examples from both Canada and the United States, I examine the role of craft breweries with respect to their (a) adaptive reuse of abandoned buildings, (b) role in neighborhood revitalization, and (c) role as neighborhood Third Places.

Adaptive Reuse

Adaptive reuse is a "process of retrofitting old buildings for new uses, which allows structures to retain their historic integrity while providing for occupants' modern needs" (Clark, 2008). Because of adaptive reuse, craft breweries occupy buildings that were once churches, hotels, banks, etc. (Reid et al., 2019) (see also Table 2.1).

There are numerous advantages of adaptive reuse. For communities, it can alleviate urban sprawl (Lewin & Goodman, 2013), while often preserving

DOI: 10.4324/9781003371564-4

Table 2.1 Examples of adaptive reuse by craft breweries

Name	Location	Original Use	Constructed	Brewery Opened
Church Brew Works	Pittsburgh, PA	Roman Catholic Church	1902	1996
Maumee Bay Brewing Company	Toledo, OH	Hotel	1859	1995
Pavlov's Brewing Company	Temperance, MI	Bank	1992	2019
Mission Brewery	San Diego, CA	Bread Factory	1894	2007
Moontown Brewing Company	Whitestown, IN	High School Gymnasium	1941	2018
Junction Craft Brewing	Toronto, ON	Industrial Incinerator	1934	2018
Mill Street Brewery[1]	Ottawa, ON	Grist Mill	1842	2011
Little Brown Jug Brewery	Winnipeg, MB	Livery Stable for City Hall	1890	2016

Source: Various websites.

a historically valuable building (Plevoets & Van Cleempoel, 2011). Lynch (2021, p. 1) suggests the benefits of adaptive reuse extend well beyond preservation of a building, describing it as an "age-old practice designed to reimagine, remake and revitalize local economies, cities and communities," while Bullen (2007, p. 27) argues that "retaining older buildings rather than building more new ones" creates "more interesting community environments." For the beer drinker, it provides a "one-of-a-kind" venue in which to enjoy beer (Bobonick, 2022).

In seeking out a building to occupy, craft brewery entrepreneurs are often attracted to "economically peripheral" locations (Weiler, 2000, p. 168), which offer affordable real estate in the form of abandoned buildings (Mathews & Picton, 2014; Colliers International, 2015). As stated by Colicchio et al. (2019), "deindustrialized areas have an abundance of relatively cheap, underutilized real estate that is ideal for brewers since there is existing infrastructure for water, sewage and power." Inexpensive real estate can be particularly important in a brewery's formative years. For example, low rent payments were critical to the early survival of Great Lakes Brewing when it opened in the Ohio City neighborhood of Cleveland, OH in 1988 (Alexander, 2013). Some buildings occupied by craft breweries (e.g., an early 20th century church) have historic value, while others have more "vernacular origins" (e.g., a late 20th century bank) (Bullen & Love, 2011, p. 412). Whether the building is historic or modern, craft breweries are engaged in the "reclaiming of often obsolete space" (Cushman & Wakefield, 2017, p. 16).

While it appears to be common practice, no data exists enumerating the number of craft breweries in the United States that engage in adaptive reuse. According to Cushman and Wakefield (2017, p. 16), with respect to American craft breweries, there has been a "limited amount of ground-up new construction . . . but this has been a fraction of the activity that we have seen in comparison to redevelopment" of existing structures. Data does exist for Canada, where studies suggest that between 78% and 83% are located in buildings once utilized for another purpose (Mathews, 2020; Mathews & Picton, 2023). Unique spaces contribute to craft beer's success. As observed by Colliers International[2] (2015, p. 5), "craft beer is as much about getting creative with the space the brewery is located in as it is about creating unique beer recipes," while CBRE (2016, pp. 3–4), notes that:

> An adaptive reuse location can deliver a unique experience to the consumer not found in other types of conventional real estate . . . the craft beer consumer is looking for a unique atmosphere, taste, and overall experience and it is up to the breweries to meet those expectations. The physical space and its associated atmosphere play an important role in achieving the "experience" consumers have come to expect.

According to Cushman and Wakefield (2017, p. 25), "a brewery without an interesting atmosphere, no matter how many taps they have, will feel just like any other bar/restaurant. This is why both the real estate a brewery occupies and the design of the space matter immensely." Consuming a unique beer in a unique space, such as an old church or fire station provides the drinker with a unique, one-of-a-kind, experience.

While not all breweries locate in buildings with historic value, those that do play a role in their preservation (Mathews & Picton, 2014). Utilizing historic buildings contributes to a community's sense of place (Mehr & Wilkinson, 2020). As noted by Bullen and Love (2011, p. 412):

> People feel a stronger sense of connection with their local surroundings through heritage, which is quite different to the mentality associated with new building stock, in that it can be replicated anywhere and therefore lends no specific connection to the local environment. Heritage buildings are cultural icons and their preservation impacts on community well-being, sense of place and therefore social sustainability.

Brewery owners are aware of the value of locating in a historic building. Silversmith Brewing in Niagara-on-the-Lake, ON occupies a late 19th century Anglican Church. Silversmith's CEO and President, Chris Pontsioen states, "locating in a historic building brings authentic character, uniqueness, and distinction to everything we do" (Duff, 2018). For some brewery owners such as Dave Longbottom, finding an "authentic" space was as important as finding a good location. His brewery, Flora Hall Brewing is in a building that previously served as a garage/warehouse/engineering building in downtown Ottawa, ON (Duff, 2018).

In some cases, brewery owners preserve and/or reuse their building's materials. In renovating an early 20th century Catholic Church, the owners of Church Brew Works in Pittsburgh, PA retained and re-used much of the Church's original features. This included: reuse of the original pews as seating, construction of the bar using oak planks obtained from shortening the pews, restoration of the original Douglas Fir floor, refurbishment and reuse of lanterns, and bricks salvaged from the removal of the confession box to make the pillars on the outdoor sign (Church Brew Works, 2022). Relating to the church in which they are located, Silversmith's Pontsioen observes, "the real challenge of adaptive reuse in our case was ensuring the structural and aesthetic integrity of the church while ensuring the addition was functional as a brewery" (Duff, 2018). Discussing the old livery stable that houses the Little Brown Jug brewery in Winnipeg, MB, founder Kevin Selch states that their "approach taken during the construction of the brewery was to keep all the historic features that could be salvaged and update those that couldn't with modern additions" (Duff, 2018). The process of using and reusing building's existing features and materials is referred to as "material continuity" (Mars & Kohlstedt, 2020). As suggested by Bullen and Love (2011, p. 412), "the most successful adaptive reuse projects are those that respect and retain a building's heritage significance as well as add a contemporary layer that provides value for the future."

Craft breweries are credited with not only breathing life into abandoned buildings, but also into economically distressed neighborhoods. It is to that topic which I now turn.

Neighborhood Transformation[3]

Dozens of cities across North America have neighborhoods that were once hotbeds of economic activity (much of it heavy industry) during the first half of the 20th century. Many of the residents were immigrants from European countries (e.g., Germany, Hungary, and Ireland) who worked in factories such as textile and steel mills and in some cases breweries (The Canadian Encyclopedia, 2017). Unfortunately, these neighborhoods became victims of economic changes that resulted in many of their places of employment shuttered. When the jobs left, people followed. What remained were neighborhoods in disrepair. Discussing the Lawrenceville neighborhood of Pittsburgh, PA Ward (2016) notes that "with people moving out and the lack of job opportunities, crime and drugs started to invade the Lawrenceville community," while Weiler (2000, p. 173) commenting on Lower Downtown Denver, stated that "squatting and crime increased, and liquor stores (along with their entrenched customer base) became the area's most prominent resource." The NoDa neighborhood in Charlotte, NC became "known for its drug houses and prostitution" (Infanzon, 2019). In Montreal, QC, following the closure of the Lachine Canal in 1970, the city's Saint-Henri "became lined with derelict warehouses, abandoned malt silos and empty red-brick hydraulic energy stations" (García Lamarca, 2020). During the 1990s, Toronto's Parkdale neighborhood was "a deadened streetscape of mostly empty storefronts, drug deals happened in broad daylight, addicts raged and twitched, and Parkdale earned another name, Crackdale" (Whyte, 2020). Fast forward to today and, all these neighborhoods and others like them, have been transformed or are transforming into vibrant neighborhoods. These transformations have occurred because of both public and private sector investments (Alexander, 2013; Woodard, 2016). In many neighborhoods, locally owned businesses such as coffee shops, bookstores, restaurants, beauty parlors, and craft breweries have played a key role in their transformation.

The opening of a craft brewery in a distressed neighborhood can signal the start of a virtuous cycle of development. As noted by the Office of Planning and Development for the State of New York (2021, p. 2):

> The brew-pub begins to attract people to an otherwise-blighted area; as the area becomes more active, other businesses locate nearby; and this creates a more hip and vibrant atmosphere, which in turn entices more people to live in the neighborhood – usually starting with millennials and then expanding to other demographics. This process then feeds on itself in a virtuous cycle of revitalization and economic development.

In effect, craft breweries help to "reinvent declining neighborhoods" (Feeney, 2017a, p. 21). The role of craft breweries in neighborhood transformation varies by place. In some, craft breweries were "pioneer" or "first-mover" investors (Weiler, 2000). When Wynkoop Brewing Company opened its doors in 1988, it was the first major investment in Lower Downtown (LoDo) Denver in decades. As such, the brewery became an "anchor for the broader development of LoDo" (Weiler, 2000, p. 175). In a similar fashion, the opening of the Great Lakes Brewing Company in Cleveland's Ohio City neighborhood "served as a catalyst for neighborhood revitalization" (Gatrell et al., 2018). As a location for a craft brewery, both neighborhoods represented untested markets. Success, however, sent a signal to potential investors that the neighborhood was a viable business location. In discussing LoDo's transformation, Weiler (2000, p. 175) notes, "The belief was that if first-movers could be enticed to open in the district, others would follow." This happened. In both LoDo and Ohio City, other investors followed the breweries into the neighborhoods. All found homes in buildings once used for something else.

Discussing Ohio City, business owner Frank McNulty observes, "What's happening here is a bunch of small local entrepreneurs taking over a very, very defunct district full of vacancies and buildings that are hard to renovate" (Alexander, 2013). These new investors included additional breweries. Today, Ohio City is a bustling neighborhood that is home to ten breweries and a variety of other locally owned businesses (Ohio City, 2022). In addition to Wynkoop, there are two other breweries in LoDo.

In other neighborhoods, craft breweries are not pioneer investors. Rather, they invested in a neighborhood after others have started investing. For example, in the NoDa neighborhood of Charlotte, NC, craft breweries opened after other entrepreneurs invested in the neighborhood (Reid & Nilsson, 2023).

City leaders and planners recognize the role craft breweries play in transforming economically challenged neighborhoods and, as a result, facilitate their growth. As establishments that are simultaneously manufacturing and alcohol retail venues, craft breweries represent a unique zoning challenge for municipalities (Brewers' Law, 2022). This has resulted in municipalities modifying local zoning ordinances to accommodate craft breweries (Lehnert et al., 2020). As observed by Williams (2017, p. 11), "across the country . . . cities, counties and towns are battling to show they are the most craft friendly, by passing new pro-craft brewing regulations." In 2014, Anaheim, CA launched its Brew City program, with the strategic objective of making the city more craft brewery friendly. Key components of the program:

- allowed "by-right" brewery development in all commercial and industrial zones, reducing permitting time and costs,
- relaxed ordinances to better allow breweries to incorporate food services,
- strategically developed craft breweries in historic structures to boost revitalization, and
- established a "brewery concierge" planning expert to welcome the craft-beer industry and keep Anaheim on the cutting-edge of trends (Crowell, 2018).

According to John Woodhead, director of community and economic development for the City of Anaheim, the goal of the Brew City initiative was to leverage "the power of breweries to drive economic revitalization. This includes very creative re-uses of historic buildings, infusing them with an authentic sense of place" (Crowell, 2018). Between 2014 and 2022, the number of breweries in Anaheim increased from five to 21 (Smith, 2018; PubQuest, 2022). See Chapters 10 and 11 for more in-depth discussion on local ordinance changes and a case study of one city's goal of attracting breweries.

In many cities, craft brewery districts or neighborhoods have emerged, where craft breweries cluster in geographic proximity to each other. Examples include the neighborhoods: Ohio City in Cleveland, OH (10 breweries),

RiNo in Denver, CO (10 breweries), NoDa in Charlotte, NC (11 breweries), Ballard in Seattle, WA (11 breweries), and Manchester in Calgary, AB (10 breweries). Craft brewery districts are advantageous for both breweries and consumers. The former can leverage agglomeration economies, while the latter can visit several breweries in the space of an afternoon or evening (Nilsson et al., 2018). Discussing Denver's River North neighborhood, Gorski (2015) observes:

the emergence of Denver's craft brewing district means drinkers can sample several tap rooms, including on foot or by bike. That is a great advantage for breweries hoping to lure new customers, but it also means there is no room to hide if the beer doesn't measure up. Breweries need to be on their game because customers have options.

Visitor and Convention Bureaus include craft brewery districts when marketing of their city as a tourist destination (see Chapter 4 for more on beer tourism). For example, VisitCalgary.com (2022) includes a page titled "Calgary's Brewery Districts," which entices potential visitors with the following language:

With more than 40 breweries and counting, Calgary has exploded into a brewery-hopping hotspot. Beer-lovers in the know are flocking to secret areas of the city, where clusters of small breweries are growing into communities of their own and offering rewarding adventures for those willing to go beer hunting. Calgary's most prolific brewery cluster [Manchester neighborhood] has grown just south of the downtown area, with 10 breweries producing an astonishing number of award-winning brews, all within walking distance.

While craft breweries attract tourists (Plummer et al., 2005; Reid, 2018), they can also serve as community gathering spots (Third Places) for local residents. In the next section, I examine the role of craft breweries as community Third Places.

Third Places

In 1989, Ray Oldenburg, an urban sociologist, published a book titled The Great Good Place. The book's subtitle was Cafes, Coffee Shops, Bookstores, Bars, Hair Salons, and Other Hangouts at the Heart of a Community. What Oldenburg was describing in his book were Third Places; community gathering spots, where friends and family come together, relax, and enjoy each other's company. Third Places exist in contrast to homes (First Places) and work spaces (Second Places). Oldenburg identified key characteristics of Third

Places. For example, they are inclusive neutral meeting places where everyone is welcome, and conversation is the main activity (Oldenburg, 1989). They have regular customers for whom the Third Place is a home away from home.

Third Places play an important societal role, contributing to the establishment and maintenance of social networks. Their existence is indicative of a healthy and cohesive community (Bolet, 2021). As functional enablers of social interaction, Third Places generate "collective feelings of civic pride, acceptance of diversity, trust, civility, and overall sense of togetherness within a locale through sustained use and connection among residents" (Finlay et al., 2019, p. 1).

In his book, Oldenburg devotes three chapters to types of Third Places that served beer – the German beer garden in 19th century America, the English Pub, and the American tavern. Beer has a long history as a social lubricant, so it is not surprising that places that sell beer play a prominent role in his discussion of Third Places. There are both individual and societal benefits of moderate beer consumption in communal settings. Discussing the benefits of visiting the same pub on a regular basis, Dunbar and his colleagues conclude that "individuals who have a 'local' that they visit on a regular basis are more socially engaged, feel more contented in their lives, and are more likely to trust other members of their community" (Dunbar et al., 2017, p. 128). Social networks, established and nurtured in pubs and other Third Places, "provide us with the single most important buffer against mental and physical illness" (Dunbar et al., 2017, p. 126). Writing in the early 1980s Oldenburg and Brissett (1982) identified the tavern or bar as the dominant Third Place in American society. In recent decades, the number of drinking places in the United States has decreased, from 52,757 in 1993 to 39,129 in 2020 (US Bureau of the Census, 1995, 2022). This is reflective of a larger trend manifested in the decline in the number of other types of Third Places, such as places of worship and personal services (e.g. barbershops, and beauty salons) (Finlay et al., 2019). The decline of Third Places has negative societal implications by increasing stress, loneliness, and isolation, while contributing to increased crime, addiction, and sociopolitical polarization (Bolet, 2021).

Several academics and practitioners suggest that craft breweries are a new type of Third Place (Kickert, 2021; Jolly et al., 2021). George Homewood, Norfolk, Virginia's director of planning and community development, suggests craft breweries are "gathering places that are in many ways replacing things like libraries and recreation centers within a neighborhood," while Morrison (2017) describes craft breweries as "the evening analog to the third place of the morning, the coffeehouse."

Some brewery owners, inspired by Oldenburg's work, have strategically positioned their breweries as neighborhood Third Places. Colin Rath, co-owner of Migration Brewing, in Portland, OR states that his brewery is "a place for the community to come together" (Oregon Brewing Running Series, 2017), while Dave Longbottom of Flora Brewing Company in Ottawa, ON envisions his brewery becoming "a permanent neighbourhood gathering spot."

In addition to providing a place to gather and enjoy a beer, craft breweries also function as flexible community space, hosting events such as yoga classes (Strohacker et al., 2021), religious worship services (Chitwood, 2019), and a dads/kids group meeting space (PDX/Portland Dads Group, 2022). Some promote physical activities by organizing running and bicycling groups (Stocker et al., 2021).

Craft breweries also tend to be family-friendly, with both children and dogs welcome. As noted by Hancock et al. (2018, p. 3), "while breweries have a reputation for attracting young people . . . they appeal to families as well. They provide an atmosphere that is comfortable for parents and their children to eat and enjoy social time with others." Not all craft brewery patrons are happy to see children in taprooms, especially when abdicate their parenting responsibilities to other adults and/or taproom staff (Crouch, 2018; Holl, 2018; Nurin, 2018). Some have responded by banning children or limiting the hours when they can be in their taproom (Backus, 2019; Mirabella, 2018).

Conclusion

While I have painted a positive picture of craft breweries in this chapter, it would be remiss of me not to acknowledge what many consider the dark side of neighborhood transformation (i.e., gentrification). There is a large literature on the negative aspects of gentrification (see for example Smith et al., 2020; Zuk et al., 2018; Walks & Maaranen, 2008), which includes the displacement of poorer residents and businesses partly because of rising property values. In some neighborhoods such as Over-the-Rhine in Cincinnati, OH and Parkdale in Toronto, ON, residents have protested and pushed back against gentrification (Woodward, 2016; Reid et al., 2020; Whyte, 2020). See Chapter 5 for further research.

Despite misgivings regarding neighborhood gentrification, the process generally continues largely unabated. Craft breweries are an important part of a neighborhood transformation in many cities across North America. City planners and others dedicated to improving their cities consider the opening of a craft brewery in a neighborhood a positive development. As a result, many have modified zoning ordinances to accommodate the locational needs of craft breweries. Craft brewery owners in search of inexpensive real estate have embraced abandoned buildings in economically distressed neighborhoods. Through the process of adaptive reuse, they occupy and breathe new life into abandoned buildings, some of which have historical value. As many abandoned buildings are in economically distressed neighborhoods, their rebirth as craft breweries often contribute to neighborhood transformation. In some neighborhoods, breweries are pioneer investors, functioning as a catalyst for subsequent investment. In other neighborhoods, craft breweries enter neighborhoods after the revitalization process has started. While craft breweries are destinations for beer tourists, many also serve as community Third Places, thereby providing a neighborhood gathering spot for friends and neighbors to gather.

Acknowledgment

I would like to thank Brian Bastien for sharing so generously his insights on the Canadian craft brewing industry.

Notes

1 In 2015, Labatt Brewing Company (owned by Anheuser-Busch InBev) purchased Mill Street Brewery.
2 Colliers International, CBRE, and Cushman and Wakefield are commercial real estate companies that work with the craft brewing industry.
3 While the term "transformation" is in the section's title, I recognize that alternatives such as "gentrification" or "revitalization" exist.

3 The Regional Impact of Craft Breweries

Local Workforce Development and Economic Growth

Vince Vasquez

How has the growing footprint of the craft beer industry in the United States impacted regional workforce and economic planning? With the rise of craft breweries and brewpubs across the country in the early 21st century, metropolitan regions have experienced steady industry activity and development, and unique industry clusters have emerged that draw talent and collaborative energy. Understanding why breweries and brewery jobs matter from an economic development perspective can help convey the unique opportunities they offer to those aiming to build meaningful career pathways and solutions for civic and business development.

Local economic development is a recognized process by which the "public sector, business and civil society work collectively to create better conditions for economic growth and employment generation. Its purpose is to build up the economic capacity of a local area to improve its economic future and the quality of life for all" (Villanueva, 2014). Scarce resources (labor, land, and capital) are allocated and leveraged to increase economic activity and improve workforce and business outcomes. Elected officials and community stakeholders (chambers of commerce, citizen advisory boards, colleges and universities, etc.) work together to set economic development goals, develop strategies to reach those goals, and craft public–private partnerships as needed to facilitate greater investment, entrepreneurial activity, and job creation. Priority goals that are commonly set in this process include increasing jobs and the local tax base, environmental sustainability, and social equity. Common barriers to economic development faced by cities include the lack of land or buildings available, high cost of land, lack of skilled labor or high labor costs, lack of capital, and inadequate public infrastructure.

As public policymakers evaluate changing or updating their economic development goals and strategies, greater consideration should be given to formally incorporating the craft brewing industry into their plans. As I will demonstrate, craft breweries and brewpubs serve more community needs than just a frosty pint or a warm meal – they also foster meaningful career pathways and economic benefits that extend beyond dollars and cents.

DOI: 10.4324/9781003371564-5

Workforce

Arguably, breweries are aligned with many of the job creation goals set by economic development managers. Chiefly among them, brewery jobs are growing, and job growth has been steady over the past decade. According to the most current data available from the US Bureau of Labor Statistics, there were 108,111 brewery jobs in the United States in June 2022, a 36% increase in jobs from four years prior (79,627 in June 2018. It is important to note that the Brewers Association counts a larger industry workforce figure using a different methodology [Bureau of Labor Statistics, 2018]).

To be sure, breweries comprise only a small fraction of the entire 131.1 million non-farm private sector workforce in the United States (Bureau of Labor Statistics, 2022), but direct industry employment is only one dimension of job growth linked to craft beer. As beverage manufacturers, breweries have one of the largest employment "multiplier effects" found in economic research, catalyzing local job growth across multiple sectors with each industry dollar spent. A multiplier effect is the economic output created when new dollars are recirculated in an economy, creating and supporting ancillary jobs and business activities in a defined geographic area. Multiplier effects include the economic changes that result as businesses procure goods and services from other businesses (and, in turn, these businesses buy goods and services from others), as well as when workers spend their wages on goods and services, all of which can be quantified as new indirect jobs created. Beverage manufacturing draws heavily from local service providers and suppliers for product ingredients, sales, and distribution; it is estimated that for every 100 direct beverage manufacturing jobs, 473.8 indirect jobs are created (Bivens, 2019). This employment multiplier ratio ranks in the top quintile of all 179 major private employment sectors analyzed.

Multiplier ratios also tell a lot about an industry's overall "economic impact," or the total financial value of its key economic relationships in a geographic area (jobs created directly and indirectly, capital spent, sales, etc.). Economists use econometric modeling software to evaluate multiplier ratios, crunch the numbers, and calculate economic impact data points. This type of research is helpful for economic planning purposes and for when major civic decisions must be made on where to allocate scarce public resources. The economic magnitude of craft beer capital spreads far and wide in the national economy; the Brewers Association calculates the total economic impact of the 2021 US craft brewing industry to be $76.3 billion, creating 170,000 direct jobs and supporting a total of 490,000 jobs nationwide (Watson, 2022).

Industry occupations focus on manufacturing, hospitality, packaging, distribution, management, quality control, sanitation, and sales and marketing, all of which are transferable skills within and outside of the brewing business.

Some of the more common occupations found at craft breweries (and their general roles and responsibilities) include:

- Production

    - Cellarman/Cellar Worker: monitoring the fermentation and brewing process, clean-in-place cleaning and sanitation of kegs and brewing equipment, and assisting team with other tasks related to beer production;
    - Brewing Technician/Quality Assurance/Quality Control: collecting and analyzing quality control data, including in-process and post-production quality control; operating canning and kegging line; and packaging duties;
    - Brewer: operates brewhouse equipment and produces beer, measures and combines raw ingredients, maintains inventory records and other management, and safety and analysis duties;
    - Head Brewer: oversees all brewing operations at the brewery; manages recipes, fermentation and yeast handling, and carbonation; orders ingredients and equipment; manages brewery staff; and other safety, sanitation, and quality assurance duties.

- Tasting Room

    - Bartender/Beertender/Server: takes beverage orders; serves beer; cleans glassware, equipment, and tasting-room area; operates a cash register/point of sale purchase system; and restocks supplies;
    - Tasting Room/Front of House Manager: supervising the work of bartenders, managing customer relations, helping with staff duties, developing programs and strategies to increase sales and tasting-room attendance, and other managerial and administrative duties.

- Administration

    - Brewery Manager: oversees all brewery staff, creates work schedules, works with Head Brewer on key performance indicators (KPIs) for beer production, upholds safety standards, and evaluates employee performance;
    - Accountant/Human Resources/Marketing/Graphic Design/Events: these positions may be on a contract basis, depending on the size of the brewery.

- Sales

    - Delivery/Truck Driver: driving a commercial truck or van to deliver beer and merchandise along an established route, collecting payment from customers, picking up empty kegs, and following safety protocol and safe driving procedures;

- Sales Representative: selling beer and other brewery products to current customer accounts, increasing the number of customer accounts and generating higher sales volume, and other marketing and customer relations duties.

There are some important distinctions on industry wages to be made based on the geography and size of the brewery (which we won't delve into here), but the overall wage data provides a meaningful baseline. Many of the industry jobs on the beer production side are categorized by the federal government under the beverage manufacturing occupational category known as "Separating, Filtering, Clarifying, Precipitating, and Still Machine Setters, Operators, and Tenders" (Standard Occupational Classification Code 51–9012). In May 2021, this occupational category had an annual average wage of $48,180 a year, with a 25th percentile to 75th percentile annual wage range of $36,650–$57,690. For comparison, the Bureau of Labor Statistics calculates the May 2021 annual mean wage for all occupations in the United States as $58,260.

For the cellarman position, Glassdoor identified an average salary of $45,837 per year, with a $31,000–$78,000 possible salary range, and a "most likely range" of $39,000–$63,000 (between the 25th and 75th percentile of all pay data available). For brewing technicians, the salary range was $32,000 to $63,000, with $37,000–$53,000 as the most likely range and $42,222 as the average annual salary. Brewery managers make $58,620 in average annual base pay, with a range of $42,000 to $100,000 and a most likely range between $52,000 and $81,000. Finally, for the brewer occupation, Glassdoor provided a range of $35,000–$92,000, with a most likely wage range between $44,000 and $73,000 and $52,150 as the average annual salary.

Most jobs at breweries and brewpubs fit squarely into the middle-skill jobs portion of the workforce – they require more education than a high school diploma but less than a four-year college degree. The middle-skill population in the country is sizeable – according to the 2021 American Community Survey, there were approximately 44 million Americans aged 25 years or older with some college education but no college degree, which is about one out of five Americans (19.3%) in this age range (US Census Bureau, 2021). Middle-skill jobs were traditionally a gateway to higher paying and more skilled work, but due to years of stagnant wages, globalization, and the effects of technology and business automation, they have dwindled and become a smaller portion of our domestic workforce, as the number of low-skilled and high-skilled jobs have grown, respectively:

In 1980, non-college workers were evenly split between low- and medium-paid occupations (at 42 percent and 43 percent, respectively) and the remaining one-seventh of workers without college degrees were in traditionally high-paid occupations. By 2016, the share of non-college educated workers in mid-pay occupations had fallen to 29 percent, with about 12 of the overall 14 percentage point decline representing a shift to the low-paid category and less than a 1.5 percentage point increase in the high-pay category.

(Autor, 2022)

What is interesting to note is that this phenomenon is not limited to the United States; indeed, there is evidence of a shrinking middle-skill workforce across many industrialized countries in Europe. The Organization for Economic Cooperation and Development (OECD) summarized workforce data from the United States and other industrialized nations:

> Some jobs are increasingly failing to deliver on the promise of the status they have traditionally been associated with. In particular, middle-skilled workers are less likely than previously to make it to the middle-income class . . . in terms of job polarization, most countries are not so much faced with a "middle class problem," but rather with a "middle skill" problem, as workers in this group are now less likely to be in the middle-income class. These changes may help explain some of the social frustration which has been at the centre of the political debate even in countries where the size of the middle-income class has remained stable.

(OECD, 2019)

The resulting "hourglass economy" endangers public efforts to curb income inequality, particularly at a time of soaring inflation and high cost of living. Compounding matters, many of the common workforce-related challenges that brewery owners face today are similar to those of other non-brewing middle-skill employers – mediocre wages and benefits, lackluster work conditions, and struggles to recruit and retain talented, qualified workers, particularly since the pandemic. *Brewery jobs, despite all of their growth and promise, need help, and learning how to strengthen industry career pathways may provide lessons across the middle-skill workforce.* With this in mind, it makes logical sense for vulnerable brewery jobs to be folded into the targeted solutions to improve all middle-skill jobs and the middle-class families they support – apprenticeships, skills-based hiring, and educational partnerships.

Apprenticeships

Today, there are critical skills and knowledge gaps in the US workforce that are impeding greater economic growth and mobility. Workers are missing opportunities for career advancement and higher wages for in-demand jobs, while businesses are struggling to hire qualified candidates, particularly for middle-skilled and high-skilled work. One solution to help resolve these issues is to create more apprenticeship programs. Paid, experiential learning that combines classroom and jobsite instruction with mentorship helps build career readiness, professional development, and in-demand skill sets. Apprenticeships assist employers with recruiting and retaining skilled workers and improving their productivity in a cost-effective way. Through apprenticeship programs, businesses can reduce their liability costs and increase their overall profitability. Workers can increase their earning potential and employability through customized, real-world, on-the-job training and work experience. As an alternative workforce education program, apprenticeships reduce the need for workers to enroll in traditional schooling programs that may require years to complete or tens of thousands of dollars in student loan debt to participate. Once limited to the traditional skilled trades such as carpentry and electrical work, public funding and programs are now emerging for nontraditional apprenticeships, due mostly to employer demand for more workers with technical training and soft skills (Ryder, 2022).

Already, breweries are working with states to strengthen and expand industry talent pipelines. Massachusetts, Montana, New York, and Michigan all have "brewers" as eligible occupations to participate in state-registered apprenticeship programs, allowing local breweries to sponsor apprentices and schools, mostly community colleges, to offer brewing education. West Virginia, which is not known for craft breweries, went one step further and in 2020 partnered with the US Department of Labor (DOL) Office of Apprenticeship and Bridge Valley Community and Technical College to create one of the few DOL-registered Brewers Apprenticeship programs in America. Their ambitious effort was focused on building a homegrown industry training program to stop the flow of brewing students enrolling in expensive out-of-state programs and offer local breweries opportunities to reskill and upskill current employees (West Virginia Department of Commerce, 2020). In addition to helping economically at-risk communities, apprenticeships can also lead to partnerships supporting vulnerable populations. Out of Bounds Nation Second Chance Initiative, a nonprofit focused on providing justice-involved individuals with education and workforce opportunities, has teamed with Riverside-based Prison Break Brewery and San Diego State University to offer a post-release craft beer apprenticeship program for up to 250 justice-involved individuals based in Southern California (Prison Break Brewery, 2022). The DOL-recognized apprenticeship program, which focuses on direct employment to three industry positions (beer sales representative, sales director, and warehouse manager) includes six to eight months in online courses, followed by six to nine months of on-the-job training and employment, all paid. Candidates must be formerly incarcerated, justice-impacted, or justice-involved. Long-term plans include scaling the apprenticeship program and expanding it across the country.

Skills-Based Hiring

As policymakers seek to support middle-skill career pathways, one challenge is reconciling the legacy effects of credentialism and degree inflation in private- and public-sector hiring practices. The widespread practice of stipulating four-year college degrees and industry credentials for middle-skill and high-skill occupations that previously did not require them began during the Great Recession, when there were more Americans seeking work than available jobs, and employers became more selective in their hiring requirements without substantively changing the jobs themselves (Bureau of Labor Statistics, 2022). College degrees were used by recruiters and human resource managers as an indicator, a proxy for soft skills and competencies acquired by workers. Research from Harvard Business School has found that this practice has resulted in an artificial talent shortage, with college-degree holders experiencing higher rates of workforce turnover and lower productivity levels and fewer employment opportunities for workers without college degrees but who may have desirable skills and/or work experience (Fuller & Raman, 2017). The pandemic has only exacerbated this issue, where there are now more job openings than job seekers (Bureau of Labor Statistics, 2022), and employers are scrambling to fill vacant positions (Fuller et al., 2022).

As a result, many businesses, particularly larger employers and tech companies, have undergone a "degree reset," eliminating degree requirements and shifting to skills-based hiring practices, now offering job applicants detailed skill descriptions under job qualifications in their job postings. When implemented, skills-based hiring has been found to widen the job candidate pool, increase time-to-hire, and foster greater workforce diversity (Chorna, 2022). As to how many breweries in the United States need to undergo a degree reset is unknown, but probably not many – it is rare to find a college degree or industry credential requirement to apply for a position at a brewery, and few entry-level positions at breweries require more than a high school diploma. Most industry workers learn skills through on-the-job training or home brewing. Still, breweries and all middle-skill employers should put in the work to review and rewrite their job descriptions and emphasize both the soft and hard skills required for the positions. Policymakers also have a role to play here – they can encourage their brewing community or local brewer's guild to develop comprehensive job descriptions and shared definitions to provide clarity to jobseekers and a common language for brewery HR managers to work from, resulting in a more efficient and effective process (Burrowes et al., 2014). Local leaders should also ask business owners which hard skills are lacking in the workforce and collaborate with them to develop formal educational partnerships with community colleges, four-year institutions, and/or technical schools to train for those missing skills and high-demand industry roles.

Educational Partnerships

Brewery workers that receive formal industry education today usually receive it from one of four available Cicerone Certification programs. Founded in 2008, the Cicerone® Certification Program was established to increase workforce education and introduce expert craft beer stewards throughout the world. The program seeks to replicate what sommelier training provides the wine industry – a trained professional who is knowledgeable in an artisanal food product, which they can proficiently serve to the public. Program participants are not limited to brewery employees – other employers listed on the Cicerone directory include bars, restaurants, hotels, and tourism destinations. With affordable learning modules available online, Cicerone programs have proven popular; as of December 2022, more than 130,000 US workers have completed a Cicerone program.

To be sure, interest in education programs at traditional colleges and universities is increasing; one count identifies 32 colleges and universities across 18 states actively offering industry-related courses and programs (Beer Info, 2020). These include undergraduate and extended learning certificate programs, associates, and bachelor's degree programs in fermentation science, brewing, and brewery management and brewpub operations. Many of these programs are developed in collaboration with, and at the request of, local breweries interested in affordable, accessible short-term workforce training and education programs to develop "grow your own" industry career pathways.

The variety of industry education programs underscores the spectrum of industry career paths and strong demand for skilled and trained workers. Consider the case of San Diego County, one of the nation's largest craft beer industry clusters and home to four unique industry certificate programs: San Diego State University (SDSU) Global Campus Professional Certificate in the Business of Craft Beer, University of California San Diego (UCSD) Extension Professional Certificate in Brewing, California State University San Marcos (CSUSM) Extended Learning EngiBeering Certificate, and MiraCosta College BrewTech Program. The curriculum for the UCSD Professional Certificate in Brewing focuses heavily on fermentation science and brewing technology and has math and science prerequisites for program participants (UC San Diego, 2022). This 26-quarter unit program has online and in-person courses and requires a 90-hour internship at a brewery. Conversely, the SDSU Certificate program is "ideal for those who wish to build careers outside of brewing," with coursework preparing students for employment "in both Front of House and Back of House operations" (SDSU, 2022). SDSU curriculum focuses on hospitality management, marketing and sales, and draught system safety and maintenance. On the more generalized side, CSUSM's Engineering Certificate is designed for both the industry hobbyists seeking educational enrichment and industry professionals focused on career advancement (CSUSM, 2022). Courses in this 12-course program were created in collaboration with regional brewers and include industry history, sensory evaluation, and electives on brewing materials and industry entrepreneurship. Finally, the 280-hour MiraCosta BrewTech Program enrolls two cohorts a year and can be completed in 15 weeks, leading students to direct employment as brewery technicians (MiraCosta College, 2022). Students gain hands-on experience from an on-site, one-barrel brewing system; receive OSHA and LEAN certification; and must complete an 80-hour internship. It is the first and only program at a community college to be certified by the Master Brewers Association of the Americas, which has rigorous industry curriculum standards (California Community College Chancellor's Office, 2022).

Economic Growth

Beyond workforce needs, breweries offer a meaningful way for communities to grow their economic base in ways other businesses cannot, particularly for those communities that are small, rural, or economically distressed. One brewery among many in a metropolitan city of 600,000 may not have as much magnitude or ripple effect economically as say a single brewery in a town of 30,000 or located somewhere far from the urban core.

Consider the Rincon Band of Luiseño Indians, a Native American tribe that occupies a 5,000-acre reservation in Valley Center, a rural unincorporated area located in the northeastern part of San Diego County, more than an hour's drive by car from downtown San Diego. The Rincon Band has a tribal population of 500 enrolled members (Mapp, 2023). Part of the tribe's mission is to generate a revenue stream to fund its own government services, such as health and social services, a tribal court, and recreational programs. The Rincon Band not only owns a casino and receives gaming profits from visitors, but also seeks to expand its portfolio of commercial enterprises through the Rincon Economic Development Corporation (REDCO), which it launched in 2009 to promote economic development. After opening a gas station and convenience store in 2012, REDCO set out to establish a craft brewery, to take advantage of the market trend and consumer interest in craft beer. Revenue earned from operating a brewery captures revenue lost at the casino and gas station selling other people's beer and expands on-premise and off-premise alcohol sales beyond the preferences of casino visitors. In 2016, REDCO opened the first tribally owned and operated brewery located on tribal land in Southern California, which has been renamed and is currently known as the Rincon Reservation Road (3R) Brewery.

According to REDCO Board Chairman Rik Mazzetti, 3R is an opportunity not only to generate revenue but also to share tribal culture (the beers and tasting rooms incorporate tribal history, colors, and themes) and help build community relationships; a portion of the revenue earned goes toward the tribe's grants program, supporting numerous local nonprofit organizations throughout the region. Sustainability is also a priority for 3R; in addition to sourcing their brewing water from their own aquifer, REDCO is looking to establish 10 acres on their reservation for a future hop farm. Spent grain from the brewing process are also sent to Native American-owned cattle ranches to be used as livestock feed. That 3R has such an outsized business operation despite being from such a small community is by design. "This is paramount for us, giving back to our tribe," Mazzetti says, "Not only on a monetary basis, but that the product is something we can be proud of . . . we want everyone on the reservation to be proud to say, it's our beer, it's Indian-owned, it's 100% from ingredients on the reservation. We're very happy about that" (Newman, 2022).

Today, 3R brews eight core beers as well as seasonal beers, all of which are available on tap at a tasting room located on the reservation, in their tribe's casino, and at a tasting room they opened in early 2022 in the coastal San Diego neighborhood of Ocean Beach. The tribe's canned beer is distributed widely and is now available at Costco, BevMo!, about two dozen restaurants and liquor stores in Southern California (including casinos and businesses owned by other tribes), and Disneyland Park.

In communities of all sizes, breweries can offer value for community and economic development that other types of top-tier business sectors cannot. For example, breweries generate sales tax revenue from beer, food, and merchandise sales. Sales tax is one of the largest general fund revenue sources for municipalities, and it pays for roads and other traditional public services such as police and fire, parks, and libraries. With potentially millions of dollars in annual revenue, breweries can be lucrative for the cities in which they locate. Other manufacturing-type businesses commonly found on industrial-zoned land or in industrial parks do not generate sales tax revenue, such as software, biotech, and life science companies. When important public decisions have to be made about the use of scarce industrialized land, or permit approvals for brewery expansions are in question, what a business will do for the local tax base is an important consideration that should not be ignored.

It's also worth pointing out that financial success for a brewery translates into a larger geographic footprint in a community, not a smaller one. Greater demand for craft beer from a brewery means raising the roofline in the brewery to make space for larger fermenters and brite tanks; next-door properties may be purchased or leased to expand the size of the tasting room, and satellite tasting rooms are opened throughout the region. The same cannot be said for other types of businesses, particularly those like research and development, pharmaceutical companies, and others creating intellectual property, which may have a business model based on being acquired by a large market-leading corporation, which may be out-of-state or out of the region. For those businesses, success is the final sale for their intellectual property, some job transfers to the larger company (wherever it is located), and paying back lenders and financial investors. Their local geographic footprint shrinks, not grows.

Conclusion

Brewery jobs matter because they are fast-growing, middle-skill, middle class jobs, which are growing scarce in today's economy but are an essential part of building a strong, equitable economy. For brewery jobs not to experience the same pitfalls that have led to so many disappearing middle-skill jobs in the United States, breweries and communities need to work together to build solutions to strengthen and grow brewery jobs, chiefly through apprenticeships, skills-based hiring, and educational partnerships. Beyond creating jobs, breweries can make other meaningful and unique economic contributions to communities big and small.

If community leaders and brewery owners can find ways to partner and improve the prospects for brewery career paths, they will be building resilience into the local middle-class workforce, one more prepared for the challenges of the 21st century.

4 Beer Cities and Ale Trails

Patterns and Practices in Craft Beer Tourism

Gail Ann Williams and Steve Shapiro

Defining and Studying Craft Beer Tourism

As 21st century craft beer production has increased dramatically across the United States and the rest of world, so too has research into craft beer tourism (CBT). Many researchers favor a narrow definition for beer tourism. One of the earliest studies defined beer tourism "as visitation to breweries, beer festivals and beer shows for which beer tasting and experiencing the attributes of beer regions are the prime motivating factors for visitors" (Plummer et al., 2005, p. 449). The growth of CBT is no longer a North American phenomenon; craft breweries, festivals, beer cities, and ale trails in their roles continue to attract visitor attention in Europe, South America, Africa, and Asia (Cabras et al., 2020, pp. 739–750; Bizinelli et al., 2013, pp. 349–375; İsildar et al., 2020, pp. 209–219; Hermann et al., 2019, pp. 18–30; Chirakranont & Sunanta, 2021, p. 10448). The phenomenon is global and academic interest has followed as craft breweries have spread.

The formal study of CBT incorporates the use of a range of tourism concepts and frameworks such as neolocalism, experiential tourism, and cultural omnivore theory which may provide useful insights to practitioners in planning, brewery management, destination marketing, and the tourism industry. Neolocalism is an "effort by businesses to foster a sense of place based on attributes of their community" (Holtkamp et al., 2016, p. 66). The associated brand storytelling may reference local landmarks, the personalities of local brewery founders, or a location in an historic building. In many cases, the perception of authenticity is not tied to local ingredients in the liquid, but "in the context of craft beer, terroir or taste of place, is more a matter of social ties to place and community– social terroir– than to the specific natural resource characteristics of any particular place" (Sjölander-Lindqvist et al., 2019, p. 151).

Urban breweries may want to inform their outreach strategies by seeing visits to their taprooms as part of the 'city tourism' pattern, characterized by travelers using communications technologies such as mobile phones who are drawn to destinations not intended for tourists, allowing these visitors more interaction with residents (Bock, 2015, pp. 1–8).

DOI: 10.4324/9781003371564-6

Another framework for investigation is Cultural Omnivore Theory. While tastes were once typically categorized as lowbrow or highbrow, for more than three decades observers have been reporting that traditional highbrow preferences are now increasingly incorporated with an eagerness to experience a full range of expressions of culture, including food and beverages. Beer tourists fit into this omnivorous category, seeking quality beer but adding on memorable active experiences such as visits to noted restaurants, food trucks, farmers' markets, wineries, and local cultural events along with their beer-centric itineraries. "Compared to travelers who have not been motivated by beer, beer tourists are more likely to participate in nearly every type of food and beverage travel activity, excluding the most common or 'usual.'" (Stone et al., 2020, p. 172)

Researchers, commercial entities, and government organizations are measuring and observing "beercation" behaviors. At times, the goal of supporting CBT involves getting the reputation of specific destination breweries to be more closely aligned with their respective communities. Although such breweries may be well known, their locations may not be common knowledge outside the immediate area. From the point of view of the entities dedicated to fostering tourism, the missing link between a widely known and respected brand and the reputation of its place of origin is a powerful motivator for public-private research, such as reacting to "a lost opportunity to market a strong asset, as there is potential for building Sonoma County as a craft beverage destination" (Sonoma Report, 2013, p. 10).

"Pliny the Younger" Pilgrims

One seasonal beer release brings thousands of visitors and millions of tourist dollars annually to Sonoma County, located in Northern California. This beer has an interesting history. According to Natalie Cilurzo, co-founder of Russian River Brewing Company (RRBC), Vinnie Cilurzo initially brewed Pliny the Younger in 2005 in response to an annual pattern of slow sales in February at their Santa Rosa brewpub (Cilurzo interview). This seasonal dip in demand meant that RRBC had excess brewing capacity. Brewing a slower-finishing recipe would not disrupt the production schedule for their regular beer lineup by tying up tanks as it took its time to ferment. Vinnie designed a beer he described as a "Triple IPA," with more alcohol and hops than RRBC's Double IPA, "Pliny the Elder," and called it "Pliny the Younger." Younger was produced and released annually without much fanfare until 2010.

Nobody cared. And then in 2010 . . . That was the first year that we had a line down the sidewalk. We didn't know that Beer Advocate and Rate-Beer.com beer enthusiasts were rating beers around the world. Beers that

I guess they had had – or never had – I'm not really sure. But Pliny the Younger was rated as one of the best beers in the world in 2010.

(Cilurzo interview)

Trying to provide a less chaotic customer experience, over the following years RRBC adopted practices that also made the Younger release more attractive to tourists. Critically, the amount of beer poured per day in the RRBC pub was rationed (Cilurzo interview) to have enough to pour for two weeks on premise, after setting aside some kegs designated to go into distribution at select bars and events, including SF Beer Week, founded in 2009. (Brooks, 2013, p. 107) Allocating a specific quantity per day meant visitors to RRBC could count on beer being available if they got a good position in the line outside of the establishment. In addition, the brewery instituted custom wristbands for all participants to manage the number of pours each patron could order and meter the total number admitted to the crowded pub at any one time (Cilurzo interview).

In 2013, RRBC was approached by the Sonoma County Economic Development Board (EDB), a local government agency, with a proposal to research the tourism-driven economic impact of pouring that year's batch of Younger at their brewpub over the two-week release. The study revealed that over these two weeks, there was a $2.4 million economic impact contributed by the customers who had traveled from outside the county specifically to try Younger. By polling attendees, the Sonoma EDB learned that a significant portion of the visitors who came to town for the release had stayed overnight in local hotels, and added side trips to other breweries, restaurants, and wineries. The beer tourists spent over $1.4 million directly on their visits. As is customary in such analysis, the total impact was calculated after factoring in secondary effects, such as local spending by employees who got extra shifts or tips due to the influx. While most of the tourists traveled to Sonoma County from other parts of California, 25 other US states and 5 foreign countries were represented (Sonoma County Economic Development Board, 2013).

Since then, the Pliny the Younger EDB study has been updated. Researchers found that the economic impact rose to $4.88 million in 2016, $5.1 million in 2020, and climbed to $6.1 million in 2022 after the in-person event was canceled for 2021 due to the pandemic. Accommodation spending almost tripled from 2013 to 2022, from a $165 average expenditure to a $548 lodging cost per group per visit, with an average group size of 2.7 people (Sonoma County Economic Development Board, 2022). To assist with the rising costs of local accommodations, RRBC arranges special hotel rates at Sonoma County hotels, advertising the discounts on their website and social media accounts. In 2022, they helped book 282 rooms directly related to the Younger release (Cilurzo interview).

According to the EDB's Aleena Decker, the major impetus for the initial survey in 2013 was the rapid growth in the county's breweries and craft beer sales at that time (A. Decker and N. Cheek personal communication, August 10, 2022). The Sonoma County Craft Beverage Report of 2013 reported that "As of 2013, there were 18 craft breweries in Sonoma County, with eight having opened in the last two years. The overall annual economic impact of Sonoma County's brewery industry was estimated to be $123 million in 2012" (Sonoma Report, 2013).

A major goal of the Sonoma County EDB is to gather "essential data so that businesses and policymakers can identify problems, engage in discussion, and partner to resolve issues that stand in the way of economic success for our region" (Sonoma Report, 2013). The original survey methodology required paper surveys handed to groups of attendees by RRBC staff when they were seated, to avoid any "intoxication bias." RRBC provided an incentive to complete the forms by conducting a drawing for a Pliny the Younger sweatshirt. One of the reasons the EDB has analyzed this event repeatedly has been "the strong partnership with RRBC, because it requires a lot of coordination" (A. Decker and N. Cheek personal communication, August 10, 2022). When events have short-term negative impacts apparent to people who do not attend, revealing the less visible positive economic impact can offer context. It puts to rest the question of whether "having people wrap around downtown" waiting to get into the brewpub is a nuisance side effect of people who may be benefitting the host business but perhaps not the county's residents and merchants (A. Decker and N. Cheek personal communication, August 10, 2022).

A single beer release that has captured the imaginations of beer tourists year after year is unusual within the broader umbrella of CBT. However, releases are similar to "destination" craft beer festivals in that they provide an opportunity to survey CBT visitors. A few such festivals have been studied over multiple years. For example, a survey of the Oregon Brewers Festival (OBF), an established annual festival in the city of Portland, estimated that the fest brought in $23.9 million in economic impact to the local area in 2017. Nearly half of the attendees came in from outside the Portland area. Visitors who came for OBF spent an average of $532 in town, resulting in $1.3 million in business taxes to support state and local government. As Oregon beer writer D.J. Paul reported, "two of the most significant findings unearthed by the study are the number of women (44.2%) attending the 2017 OBF, along with a precipitous decline (38%) in lodging expenditures by OBF attendees, despite a 6% increase in the percentage of out-of-town visitors" (Paul, 2017). Annual CBT events may not step up their total community economic impacts year over year. As one researcher put it, "Clearly, there has been a swell of patron pushback on lodging prices during the Oregon Brewers Festival" (Dense, 2020).

Festivals may have other positive community impacts. In the case of the OBF, rising numbers of women participants may be economically and culturally beneficial to the sustainability of the craft beer industry, which has its roots in a predominantly male cohort. According to a review of North

American studies profiling craft beer tourists, "between 60 and 66% are male" (Reid, 2021, p. 321). When female attendance tops 40%, craft beer observers and community and economic development organizations take notice. While destination events have revealed the ability to bring economic and other benefits to local communities, more research is needed to identify best practices and how specific CBT results can be repeatable for breweries and jurisdictions in the United States and elsewhere.

The Draw of Beer Cities

In 2021, an Internet poll conducted by Charlie Papazian, homebrewing author and founder of the Brewers Association, announced that Grand Rapids, Michigan was tied with Asheville, North Carolina, as "Beer City, USA." Janet Korn, Senior Vice President of Experience Grand Rapids, the Destination Marketing Organization (DMO) for the city, said they immediately embraced the designation (Korn interview).

> We just kind of grabbed on to *Beer City USA* and worked collaboratively with our brewers. We created a brand, and we created a logo. And then we created a way for people to be incentivized, if you will, to visit multiple breweries. People are still coming to town to become a "Brewsader", and they're still going to eight breweries so that they can be rewarded with a Brewsader t-shirt.
>
> (Korn interview)

Local breweries partnered with the DMO to collaboratively market their Beer City, paying what Korn described as "a modest fee" to be part of the effort. At first the Brewsader program relied on stamps in a paper passport to verify brewery visits. Eventually, they offered a mobile application to collect the check-ins at the different breweries. Brewery passports will be discussed in the next section.

Experience Grand Rapids made a major commitment to promote their city and the surrounding county as Beer City USA. One means of advertisement was highway billboards, making the assessment that there are possible beer tourists on the road, who might either detour to a brewery taproom while on a previously planned trip or decide to make a future visit specifically to try the local breweries. The DMO commissioned Anderson Economic Group to look at the CBT impacts in 2018–19, in contrast with an earlier survey in 2015 (Giedeman et al., 2015). Grand Rapids breweries attracted 94,815 beer tourists over the one-year period, up from 42,246 since the first study. Over 64% of the visitors traveled from elsewhere in Michigan, beyond the two counties closest to Grand Rapids, and about 25% came from out of state. The surveys were collected at intervals during each of the study years, including at an annual winter beer festival (Anderson Economic Group, 2019).

The total economic impact of CBT was calculated at $38.5 million, more than tripling from the $12.2 million total in the 2015 study. An average party of 4.2 visitors spent $150 on craft beer and stayed for 1.6 nights per visit during 2018–19. The total spending per party in town was $1,060. This funded 378 jobs or $9.9 million in earnings in the county, topping the 2015 numbers in every category (Anderson Economic Group, 2019, pp. 7–14).

The Beer City title may stay with Grand Rapids indefinitely. Stating that the purpose of the nonscientific popularity poll had been served, Papazian retired his annual Beer City USA competition after Grand Rapids won for the second time in 2013, pulling ahead of Asheville for a sole victory (Forbes, 2014). Residents of Asheville also continue to use the Beer City USA moniker in some scenarios, such as for a charity footrace called the Beer City Relay.

Breweries in locations with strong tourism economies that have little or no relation to travel specifically for beer will have a different relationship to CBT. According to Sam Watkins, General Manager of Valdez Brewing Company (VBC) in Valdez, Alaska, even the local population has seasonal swings when the town of 2,700 blows up to a population of 10,000 when travelers arrive in their recreational vehicles for the summer. Cruise ships had planned to add the town as a port of call in 2020 and finally came in 2022, following the COVID-19 pandemic years. The brewery's business plan and its subsequent construction, completed in 2019, were based on the prospect of serving beers to cruise ship tourists in season. Watkins describes their facility as "a very nice, clean, big taproom, with lots of space for people. And that's not for the locals" (Watkins interview). Of course, VBC does serve locals throughout the year and hosts "lots of community events," but the taproom was specifically designed for the large influxes of tourists in the summer "to come and have a good space," said Watkins. "And WiFi . . . the first place they want to go is somewhere with WiFi" (Watkins interview).

With significant distances between breweries outside Alaska's two main urban areas, Watkins noted that just going to a neighboring brewery for a collaboration brew involves an overnight stay and might be considered as tourism. For example, Valdez is a five-hour drive from the city of Anchorage (Watkins interview). Without clusters of nearby breweries in a district or along an ale trail, tourism is still central to the existence of a brewery in an isolated tourist destination, and the brewery still provides some degree of economic impact, if unquantified, to its community.

Back in the more urbanized parts of North America, breweries and other beer destinations attract both local and visiting craft beer drinkers when they offer "a concentrated area of breweries and additional similar experiences such as other alcohol-related establishments, restaurants, and entertainment venues" (Apardian et al., 2022). Cooperation between breweries and local tourism entities, in the form of coordinated efforts to inform visitors of the craft beer experiences to be found there, is a primary strategy for leveraging the benefits of CBT.

Districts, Trails, and Passes

Food and beverages produced in a specific place often claim distinctive local character absent any ingredient relationship to local geography or agriculture. This is a dimension a local craft brewery has in common with a local artisan bakery: the production processes and the customer experience may each be personal and local even if the ingredients are not. Unlike the allure of drinking at a rural estate winery, the thrill of tasting fresh beer near where some of the flavors were created in the soil is rarely a factor in CBT.

One of America's striking exceptions is experienced during visits to craft breweries in the Yakima Valley, two hours east of Seattle on the sunny side of the Cascade Range. Tasting beer in Yakima Valley not only offers compelling claims of sampling hop terroir as well as social terroir but delivers sweeping beer-related agricultural scenery. The Yakima Valley Beer Pass (YVBP) is a digital approach to an idea borrowed from wine tourism, the ale trail. According to John Cooper, President and CEO of Yakima Valley Tourism, the pass, launched in Spring 2022, is designed to encourage visitors to stop at more of the small, local breweries in the valley where 75% of America's hops are grown and to stay over, building the valley's role as a beer tourism destination (J. Cooper personal communication, August 9, 2022).

Ale trails and passport programs have been organized in urban and rural areas. The approach ranges from very ad hoc peer-to-peer cooperation between a group of breweries to public-private and non-profit partnerships such as passes organized by DMOs or brewers' associations. At its most basic level, a simple list of breweries can be described as a trail, leaving visitors to choose a route. On the other hand, a study of the mapmaking employed on beer trail websites identified over 100 trails, but discarded others because "Many local-, regional-, and state-level tourist bureaus refer to a 'beer trail,' but do not designate a path or geographic structure that encourages directed movement" (Feeney, 2017b, p. 12).

Passes that don't suggest routes may instead offer incentives akin to those in a coupon book, rewarding visitors with discounts. Beyond that, in many cases, gamification adds prizes for multi-brewery check-ins, sometimes rewarded with branded items and sometimes sweepstakes-style drawings, to encourage engagement and visits to multiple breweries.

Like the Brewsader program in Grand Rapids, the YVBP is promoted as a basic activity of the area's DMO, the Yakima Valley Tourism organization. The group is mandated to spend local taxes collected on short-term lodging to fund destination marketing. As of August 2022, the YVPB included one-time discounts at nine breweries, a distillery, two non-brewery beer halls, and a commercial beer touring service. Prizes are offered for completing eight check-ins in ninety days and for ten check-ins in one hundred and twenty days. The pass is built on a digital passport and destination marketing platform designed for DMOs. Alongside the YVBP on the website, but not integrated into it, is a three-day suggested beer tour itinerary that includes hiking and brunch suggestions along with brewery stops.

Cooper noted that the economic numbers he gets do not break out beer tourism specifically from tourist visits in general, which the State of Washington Tourism reported as $342 million in direct tourist spending in Yakima County in 2021. Overall, 2.3 million parties of tourists stayed an average of three nights, with their spending directly supporting nearly 3,000 local jobs. While the specific numbers are unknown, CBT is of obvious interest in the valley, especially when brewmasters arrive from hundreds of craft breweries to select from the new hop crop at harvest time. So far, Yakima Valley Tourism and the member breweries are embracing YVPB based primarily on positive anecdotal evidence from their taprooms. There are also promising early online metrics. By early August 2022, page views of the hop and beer sections of the Visit Yakima site had jumped from 5% to 8% of total website page views compared to the prior year, "and we haven't yet hit our busiest craft beer tourism period" (J. Cooper personal communication, August 9, 2022).

Ale trails also abound on the east coast. In a study funded by the Pennsylvania Liquor Control Board (Schmidt, 2021), six beer trails with a variety of features from around the state were examined. The report includes comments from trail administrators, including "what recommendations they might have for others who would like to establish a trail in their county." For Pennsylvania's Bucks County Ale Trail, the trail was relaunched to include gamification in May 2019. From that date through March 2021, 8,000 visitors registered and nearly 3,000 of them checked in at five or more breweries, earning an Ale Trail t-shirt.

The New York State Brewers Association (NYSBA) maintains a free mobile app that provides a highly customizable beer trail feature. Beer tourists can choose an area in NY state, make a list of breweries to check out, and designate a route on the app. Each new brewery check-in generates a digital stamp. Going to 300 or more of the 504 breweries earns a high-value prize: VIP entry for two to any craft beer festival produced by the NYSBA. According to NYSBA Executive Director Paul Leone, travelers must prove they patronized each destination either by electronic geolocation or by photographing the interior of the establishment (Leone interview).

Trails require attention and promotion to benefit their breweries. Early research on CBT in Ontario, Canada, looked at the popular Waterloo-Wellington Ale trail, which later failed, providing insights into the collapse of an initiative for lack of coordination between the breweries (Plummer et al., 2008).

The clustering of craft breweries in US cities has resulted in the emergence of brewery districts. Examples include the Lower Downtown and River North Art Districts in Denver, Colorado Pearl District in Portland, or the Ballard District in Seattle (Nilsson et al., 2018). Clustering of breweries facilitates beer tourism with clients move from brewery to brewery, being able to easily visit several breweries in one trip (Kraftchick et al., 2014). For the city, clustering facilitates marketing efforts, as they can promote a particular neighborhood or neighborhoods that have a critical mass of breweries. Several cities promote their breweries on their official tourism websites.

Supporting Craft Beer Tourism

Based on the review of the literature, the interviews for this chapter and the authors' experience as craft beer tourists and beer journalists, there are several ways to attract beer tourists to your brewery and/or community.

1. *Get actual numbers.* To get started with economic information, Aleena Decker suggested that a strong interest, a clear purpose, and motivated stakeholders as partners are helpful in launching an on-site survey initiative. In addition, there may be grant opportunities to fund some of the work in determining economic impacts (A. Decker and N. Cheek personal communication, August 10, 2022).

2. *Understand your visitors.* If you conduct your own survey, consider a QR code to get visitors to open your questionnaire. As Nina Cheek suggested, you streamline the process when you have the patrons do the initial data entry for you (A. Decker and N. Cheek personal communication, August 10, 2022). Are your visitors cultural omnivores? Experiment with recommending local attractions that have value to tourists and residents alike. For example, swap promotional information with a good local winery, or curate a list of staff favorites including breakfast spots or the best short local hikes, differentiating your insider tips from more generic tourist information found online.

3. *Seek out and tie into other kinds of special interest tourism companies or groups.* Sam Watkins from Valdez Brewing Company noted that in their vicinity, heli-skiing is a popular winter adventure with an international following, so they have co-branded and otherwise collaborated with the tour operators in what might otherwise be their off-season (Watkins interview).

4. *Inform brewery outreach strategies by observing how travelers are using mobile phones to find beer.* Survey or just ask guests about beer rating sites, tourist sites and preferred social media.

5. *Review the research.* There is an excellent list of suggestions arising from different promotional and organizational models in "Craft Beverage Trail Collaborations in Pennsylvania" (Schmidt, 2021).

An excellent review of the CBT literature can be found in "Craft beer tourism: The search for authenticity, diversity, and great beer" (Reid 317–337). There is a growing body of research related to craft beer tourism, but additional research needs to be done relating to the changing dynamics of CBT specifically as well as the role of craft breweries within the larger context of overall travel experiences. Regarding changing dynamics, there are opportunities to examine differences between wine, craft spirits, and craft beer tourists; how race and gender may inform CBT experiences; or what attributes make some beer festivals attract craft beer tourists from beyond the local area. In terms of both measurable behaviors such as spending and the subjective factors that go into attractive travel experiences, learning more about the function of craft beer experiences within general-focus vacations could be valuable. Sometimes a road trip is just a road trip, but visiting a local brewery is still a welcome enhancement.

Section III

Issues Facing Breweries and Cities

5 Craft Breweries and Gentrification

Anna Domaradzka

Introduction

The worldwide expansion of the craft brewing field is often argued to be about much more than just beer. In the related literature, issues like neighborhood change, revitalization, neolocalism, adaptive reuse, sustainability, or gentrification are coming up nearly as often as breweries opening and beer production. This is because craft breweries belong to a group of investments that instigate socioeconomic change at the neighborhood level and as such tend to polarize public opinion. As influential local actors, they well deserve the current attention of researchers, urban planners, and policymakers (Nave et al., 2022).

Craft beer is a consumer good that in the postmodern context carries a lot of intangible values and therefore creates different neighborhood effects than a regular pub. First, craft breweries rarely want to cater to the wider audience and instead focus on creating a quality, one-of-a-kind product. Second, they often pick locations that offer more space and low rent, which means targeting postindustrial or low-income zones, including disfranchised neighborhoods. Thirdly, for economically sound operations, they cannot survive by attracting the locals alone; they need tourists and distribution (Salovaara, 2021).

A specific "neighborhood clash" sometimes results from this tendency to locate in areas with big enough spaces for tanks and brewing vats, and affordable rent, as the relatively low volume of craft beer production does not allow for quick return on investment. Successful breweries tend to attract other similar businesses, creating clusters in the previously underdeveloped areas. This process draws a good deal of tourism and specialized interest connected to the industry, bringing new people to otherwise less attractive neighborhoods.

This chapter focuses on the existing research concerning the impact of craft breweries moving into neighborhoods and their relationship with gentrification processes. The link between craft breweries and gentrification is often anecdotal rather than data-driven, and authors struggle to prove direct causality (Barajas et al., 2017). Yet craft breweries remain controversial and are often associated with neighborhood change represented by their new and affluent client base.

DOI: 10.4324/9781003371564-8

Two main changes are associated with the emergence of a craft brewery – influx of "craft beer lovers" who recruit mainly from the white middle class and increased land prices and rents related to higher perceived attractiveness of the area. This reflects the neoliberal and colonial notions that are still very much ingrained in both Global North and South culture and propagated worldwide by global capitalism. As a result, creating places that are attractive to more affluent and white people increases market value of otherwise less affluent neighborhoods. This is why "gentrification by craft beer" is sometimes referred to as "new urban colonization" and a form of hegemonic practice of the privileged white elite.

On the other hand, in many places, breweries are seen as hope for redeveloping areas where no other businesses are willing to emerge or reuse old buildings with historical value. When Florida (2017) asked if craft breweries can transform the postindustrial neighborhoods in the United States, he was linking their development with the growing importance of creative class for urban revival. This thinking is often present in urban redevelopment strategies and creates a fertile ground for gentrification.

The first part of the chapter focuses on defining gentrification, and its global dimension, and then moves into reviewing the existing studies on the role of breweries in the process of neighborhood change. The subsequent sections discuss the role of breweries in the gentrification process and present the role of producers, consumers, as well as city managers in shaping patterns of craft-led neighborhood change. I conclude potential typologies of craft beer industry actors in relation to their role in urban revitalization and gentrification processes.

Gentrification and its global dimension

The term "gentrification" was coined by Ruth Glass in 1964, who observed that many of the working-class quarters of London have been "invaded by the middle classes, upper and lower", leading to increased housing and land prices, making both unaffordable for the original residents. Later, Smith and Williams defined gentrification as "the rehabilitation of working-class and derelict housing and the consequent transformation of an area into a middle-class neighborhood" (Smith & Williams, 1986, p. 1).

Therefore, gentrification generally refers to the process of housing and infrastructure upgrading that accompanies the movement of middle-class professionals into disinvested neighborhoods. This attracts businesses that cater to the new clientele but coincides with displacement of existing businesses and long-term residents, who are often poorer representatives of racial and ethnic minorities (Barajas et al., 2017).

Importantly, gentrification is no longer observed solely in western cities but has become a global phenomenon, a "gentrification generalised" (Smith, 2006). As Atkinson and Bridge (2005) point out, the geographical spread of gentrification reminds of the earlier waves of colonial expansion, moving into cities of the Global South but also cascading down to regions within the urban North. Not only are the new middle-class gentrifiers predominantly white, but also their aesthetic and cultural aspects of the process tend to assert a white Anglo appropriation of urban space. As a result, municipal governments with regeneration or revitalization strategies often involve prestigious new facilities (like museums or stadiums), which generate the so-called "Guggenheim effect" (Vicario & Martinez Monje, 2003).

While city leaders and entrepreneurs tend to see gentrification as a process that allows them to save the postindustrial areas or give new life to decaying districts, the neighborhoods' vulnerable residents often experience gentrification as a process of displacement and colonization by the more privileged classes, resulting in housing dislocation or loss, disrupted social networks, and public services that are out of sync with local needs (Atkinson, 2003).

The newcomers or gentrifiers who replace older residents are often cosmopolites who represent the "creative class" or affluent consumers looking for interesting urban experiences. In postcommunist countries and newly emerging economies, gentrifiers often consist of western expats employed by transnational corporations or Millennials from the creative sector and middle-class background. However, the extent of gentrification already raises questions about the types of gentrifiers (e.g., "main gentrifiers" like WASPs vs "marginal gentrifiers" like lone mothers) (Rose, 1984).

In terms of positive debates around gentrification, for many, it signifies a "back to the city" movement of middle-class suburbanites, related with higher walkability and new cultural and recreational infrastructure (Laska & Spain, 1980). In some cases, it allows for reviving the urban core by filling it with new amenities and therefore counteract unsustainable urban sprawl. Those positive narratives avoid the negative connotations of "gentrification" and instead focus on the interplay of spatial and social revitalization, pointing out to both local (safety, jobs, and tourism) as well as global (economic and environmental) benefits.

When analyzing the relation between gentrification and craft breweries, we have to discern the role of the brewery owners and their customers, as well as the wider context of local development strategy often championed by a specific coalition of local politicians, public administration, and private investors.

Inviting breweries in

In the last decades, numerous cities of the Global North have recognized the positive local impact of craft breweries and in response offered funds or altered municipal codes to make them easier to establish. This is why breweries became anchor points of economic development and revitalization, fueled by the place marketing of cities (Kearns & Philo, 1993) and managed by urban growth coalitions (Logan & Molotch, 1987). This notion also reflects the cities' ambition – stemming from Florida's (2003) influential writing – to lure bohemians, gays, and professionals, to ensure economic success. Craft breweries are magnets for people, and with traditional bars and community halls closing, they also become community hubs as well as drinking places. When you add the fact that craft breweries do not increase crime unlike regular bars (Nilsson et al., 2020, also see Chapter 7), a brewery seems like a perfect investment, establishing a sense of place and making people feel like they're part of something bigger, while bolstering the local economy.

There is a growing number of city managers who recognize the potential role of craft brewery clusters in fostering a much-needed neighborhood development (Reid & Gatrell, 2015; Sisson, 2017). Moore et al. (2016) observe how some communities are hoping to benefit from the growing consumer interest in craft beer and incorporate breweries and brewpubs into their plans for revitalization. Distressed neighborhoods can offer not only attractive historic and postindustrial buildings but also vacant land and underutilized infrastructure (Kim, 2016). Local policymakers are often counting on commercial revitalization of the area through rebirth of retail activity in neighborhoods previously considered unsafe (Sutton, 2010, p. 352).

Brewing in the hood

Reid (2020) points out that when the home brewers open commercial craft breweries, they tend to do so in the communities in which they live, creating a personal connection to the neighborhood. However, most breweries are now proudly and self-consciously local, using local history and imagery to promote their product. This conscious creation of place attachment that serves to create local loyalties and identities is termed neolocalism (Schnell & Reese, 2014). According to Barajas et al. (2017), brewery owners state that "neighborhood character" was either a primary or a very important reason for their location choice. They also referred to themselves as "pioneers and catalysts in neglected historic neighborhoods."

Older buildings can provide attractive locations where property availability can be otherwise limited and helps avoid tearing down of valuable urban tissue. Resulting stories of breweries that have opened in the middle of desolate and destitute neighborhoods but ended up completely revitalizing those areas are what the industry often showcases to prove its positive impact. Propagators also underline that breweries are community-focused and consciously invest in areas that are underdeveloped. In the United States, some even claim that "breweries and brewpubs are becoming the new town halls of America" (Greenville online, 2015).

With so many craft breweries explicitly viewing themselves as agents of neighborhood revitalization and change (e.g., Bartlett et al., 2013), it is useful to discern pioneer and follower investors (Reid, 2018). The former are responsible for starting the cycle of investment that revives a neighborhood. The latter arrive in a neighborhood after the revitalization process has started and "become one piece of a larger revitalization jigsaw" (Reid, 2018, p. 10). Walker and Miller (2018) measured the relationship between retail and residential gentrification by analyzing craft brewery openings in Portland, Oregon. Their findings show that craft breweries were slightly more likely to open in gentrified/gentrifying neighborhoods and often followed the process of neighborhood upgrading. In the 1990s, breweries were at the leading edge of gentrification, while breweries opening in the 2000s and after were more likely to be followers solidifying the already ongoing patterns of gentrification (Walker & Miller, 2018).

Mathews and Picton (2014) argue that craft beer works as a vehicle in the manufacture of new spaces of cultural consumption, aestheticizing the industrial past and pacifying resistance to gentrification. Breweries as artisanal producers lend legitimacy and add desirability to the development process, which makes the area more attractive for high-end housing developments. As Mathews and Picton (2014, p. 353) point out, "In this narrative of decline and renewal, the brew pub acts as an accelerant to the privately led, publicly coordinated creative destruction of the industrial past." Importantly, it is the public sector that works hand in hand with commercial developers, granting them special incentives and privileges to make sure they take up the burden of redeveloping certain areas. Craft breweries are often attractive partners in those growth coalitions.

Unlike the pioneering craft breweries that serve multistate consumers, the newer breweries producing beer solely for local consumption require less space and are not limited in their choice of location. Reacting mainly to the new wave of place-based consumers, smaller brewers are often respondents to changing local demographics rather than catalysts of urban revitalization.

This is further strengthened by the fact that current trends indicate an increasingly racially and ethnically diverse, female, and millennial demographic profile (Watson, 2018; also see Chapter 1), compared to the first wave of craft-beer drinkers who tended to be white, male, generation X-ers (Tremblay & Tremblay, 2005).

Gentrifiers are coming for a beer

Much as wine connoisseurs travel to wineries to experience "the terroir," or foodies look to experience local flavors, craft-beer drinkers seek out the local connection between their favorite beverage and the place where it was brewed. For those clients, old or industrial structures offer a unique atmosphere and a sense of place, building on the intangible value of the area's history, to create an experience of both taste and place. This is supported by Kraftchick et al. (2014) findings, which indicate that the unique beer and experience offered by craft breweries are the main motivating factors for visitors.

Bourdieu's (1984) observation that the style of consumption is often indicative of social distinction fits the current process of the growing craft beer, coffee, or foodie movement, coinciding with Millennials' coming of age (Holtkamp et al., 2016). By consuming food or drink and paying higher for goods in line with their value system (Holtkamp et al., 2016), those clients also express their identity and commitment to the environment.

The craft beer sector is an example of neo-artisanal production, which is a growing niche in urban cultural economy. Wallace (2019) describes the neo-artisanship of craft beer production as a pivotal force bringing changes to social and material space, which should not be decoupled from patterns of growing precarity among some residents' groups.

According to Pokrivčák et al. (2019), three main factors behind craft beer consumer's motivations are: 1) a new taste experience, 2) desire for more knowledge, and 3) moving away from the consumption of conventional beer. Craft beer has become a symbol of the desired quality of life and consumption in the city, seen by city governments as a selling point for middle-class residents, often moving back from the suburbs in search of an urban buzz. Such consumers appreciate having social experimentation experiences and eagerly participate in value co-creation, creating greater success and a competitive advantage for craft beer (Niemi & Kantola, 2018).

Neighborhood impact of craft breweries

Craft breweries are entangled in neighborhood change, as either pioneers of reinvestment or respondents to changing preferences and local culture (Cortright, 2002). The development of craft breweries can accelerate gentrification by relating to the industrial heritage such as unused manufacturing sites, which appeal to the elite consumers' aesthetics, while anchoring subsequent development in the neighborhood (Mathews & Picton, 2014).

In their recent study, Nilsson and Reid (2019) have found that single-family homes within half a mile of a brewery experienced a 9.3% increase in their value following the opening of the brewery. Condominiums within a half mile experienced a 3.2% increase in value. This can be explained by the fact that craft breweries have become a neighborhood amenity that is attractive for some to live within a walking distance (Apardian & Reid, 2020). This way, young professionals shape the spatial industry patterns with their lifestyle choices (Revington, 2018).

When Barajas et al. (2017) examined the relationship between craft breweries and neighborhood change, they did not attempt to present the direction of causality between craft brewery locations and neighborhood change. However, they did find that breweries were more likely to locate in neighborhoods where racial and ethnic diversity was decreasing, while the number of highly educated residents and people aged between 25 and 34 was on the rise. Baginski and Bell (2011) showed craft brewery penetration to be greatest in areas where quality of life, healthcare, cost of living, wage inequality, and education are higher, where residents are more socially tolerant, high-technology sectors are less developed, and the arts and culture scenes are weaker.

As Reid (2020) points out, craft breweries' development often goes hand in hand with investment by other businesses as well as the municipality, which has resulted in the revitalization of several historic areas around the United States. By turning neighborhoods full of abandoned buildings, crime, and other social problems into cool destinations, they become attractive for both new residents and tourists. The dark side to "craftbeerization" is that rising real estate values force the established, but often low-income, residents to leave.

What strengthens their local effect is that craft breweries tend to cluster geographically as it affords them an opportunity to collaborate and to market the neighborhood as a craft beer destination. This notion is reinforced by neolocalism patterns that translate into a tendency to seek out regional lore and attachment to place by new and old residents, as a reaction to the destruction of traditional community bonds (Shortridge, 1996, p. 10). As a result, a high value is placed on beer that is locally produced.

Typologies in relation to gentrification

This chapter concludes with a typology of craft breweries in relation to their local context. As every typology, this one consists of ideal types, highlighting specific qualities that seem to discern one brewery from the other. However, in some breweries two types of drivers may overlap or their motivation may change in time.

Communitymakers (Community Brewers) – growing from local communities, they develop commercial production as a next step from home brewing, often living in the neighborhood and brewing for locals as well as visitors; usually engaged in community organizing, charity work and co-production, or hosting local events; invest less in decor and more in keeping the doors open for all, staying responsive to the needs of visitors and locals; may invest in spaces based on their importance to the local community and its heritage.

Moneymakers (*Producers*) – intent on securing their position on the wider market and often requiring bigger production space; less interested in the local context, and willing to move to scale up production; often rely on more modern industrial structures and effective distribution network; represent the pragmatic orientation to marketing and focus on (relatively) big volume production rather than on developing local taprooms.

Placemakers (*Commodifiers*) – focused on creating a unique space and experience for customers, often investing in historical locations, reinventing the postindustrial structures and ambiance; interested in developing their surroundings and how it presents to the external visitors; often become part of a wider development coalition, joining developers or other businesses to upgrade; often invest in narratives and marketing, linking their business to local history or nature.

Tastemakers (Innovators) – concentrated on the product and developing unique taste, experimenting, using rare ingredients, or perfecting the styles; mainly target beer geeks and competition within the craft beer industry; are often technology and innovation-oriented and not interested in wider audience or big production volume.

Tourist traps – usually linked to restaurants or hotels, following the fashion of offering craft beer on site, to remain attractive to visitors; less concerned with the taste but emphasizing the freshness and local character of the brew.

While community brewers and tastemakers are rarely engaged in gentrification processes, placemakers are often pioneers of such developments, with moneymakers and tourist traps acting as followers, not specifically concerned if their success leads to negative gentrification effects.

Discussion

A popular narrative connects the emergence of craft breweries with revitalization or gentrification processes, particularly in postindustrial locations (Salovaara, 2021). Existing studies and development strategies associate craft breweries with entrepreneurship, job creation, and crafts production, leading to the revival of local economies. Researchers link craft breweries with place-making as well as growing appreciation of local ingredients and production.

While there is no need to bash all craft breweries as evil gentrifiers, it is important to recognize that not all of them support local communities or social upgrading of the neighborhood, focusing on their own success and clientele instead. Academic research, following the public discourse and earlier anecdotal evidence, supports the narrative underlining the role of craft breweries in neighborhood revitalization (Nilsson & Reid, 2019; Walker & Fox, 2018).

However, only a few studies take a critical look at their gentrifying impact (e.g., Barajas et al., 2017; Walker & Miller, 2019; Wallace, 2019), focusing on the US context. Interestingly, authors neglect the non-successful breweries and rarely differentiate between breweries prior to or after gentrification. In Europe, much less has been written on the topic, but some link craft beer consumption with wider strategies of cities marketing as creative hubs (Schroeder, 2020) or quasi villages (Salovaara, 2021). One narrative presents them as part of heritage-conscious communities, cherishing crafts and artisanal production. Another speaks of places where local people gather around hobbies or food to drink and socialize.

Most recent studies have confirmed the association among craft breweries, neolocalism, and revitalization in the multinational context. Illustrative cases include those from Argentina (Belmartino & Liseras, 2020), Australia (Watne & Hakala, 2013), Canada (Eberts, 2014), Brazil (Stocker et al., 2021), Bulgaria (Stoilova, 2020), Finland (Salovaara, 2021), Germany (Schroeder, 2020), Italy (Garavaglia, 2020; Crociata, 2020), Poland (Wojtyra, 2020), UK (Cabras, 2021), and the United States (Flack, 1997; Fletchall, 2014; Talmage et al., 2020).

Conclusion

Many of the neighborhoods in which craft breweries have located are experiencing revitalization and gentrification (Apardian & Reid, 2020). In some cases, craft breweries played the role of pioneer investors and are perceived as responsible for kick-starting the revitalization (Weiler, 2000; Alexander, 2013). In other cases, new breweries moved in following other investors and therefore contributed to strengthening the revitalization processes (Walker & Miller, 2018). Still, the resulting displacement patterns are not exactly the responsibility of breweries alone but rather of the business-minded urban governments, entangled in a fierce international or national race to lure investors and economic elites and too often buying into revanchist "no tolerance" strategies.

While some authors prefer to convey a generally positive story of craft breweries and neighborhood revitalization, the process of gentrification in economically distressed neighborhood should still be discussed (Brown-Saracino, 2010; Bates, 2013). What turn revitalization into gentrification are the rising real estate rents that displace existing residents and force smaller businesses out of the neighborhood (Yee, 2015; Woodard, 2016). What makes gentrification even more controversial is that the population forced to leave usually recruits from the minority populations, while the existing businesses are often those that provide affordable basic goods and services to residents (Woodard, 2016).

One thing that a brewery can do is to make sure it stays open to a mixed clientele, offering space for local initiatives and events and linking with smaller local businesses to protect the essence of the neighborhood. This type of social responsibility and people-mindedness seems to be present in the European context, and especially CEE (which represents a specific context and initial stage of craft breweries' development), where we observe numerous craft breweries emerging in postindustrial, rural, and tourist locations, with no pattern of gentrification yet visible. A more pressing concern seems to be the touristification, which is a growing pain in main European destinations, where the influx of tourists – many of them interested in craft culture – is highly problematic.

Therefore, the risk related to "gentrivitalization" as well as "touristification by craft beer" should be monitored, to make sure that breweries bring something positive to the neighborhood instead of instigating displacement or discomfort (Infante, 2020). This is also in the best interest of breweries, as rising real estate prices in gentrified neighborhoods already negatively affect breweries seeking to expand their operations (Chung, 2008) and discourage new breweries from joining the clusters.

Reid points out that a craft brewery does not revive the neighborhood on its own but is usually part of the bigger process. Breweries did, however, become symbols of gentrification as they are magnets for a younger demographic and people with enough disposable income to consume the expensive craft beer. While recognizing the positive role of craft breweries in neighborhood revitalization, we should not forget the "pushing out" patterns that go along racial and income lines and literally change the face of the neighborhood.

To summarize, while there seems to be sufficient proof that craft brewing businesses are good for the city's economy as they tend to invest in struggling neighborhoods and often add interesting amenities in the developing areas, our main question remains whether they are good for the communities in which they settle. One can argue that breweries bring new life to struggling neighborhoods and attract new businesses while stimulating walkable development and diverse sociocultural activities (Somerville, 2013). However, in vulnerable communities, the price of one more craft beer may be much higher than a couple of dollars.

6 Race and Equity in the Craft Brewing Industry

Omar Passons

Introduction

It is reasonable for people whose passion is beer but whose experiences have not included many interactions in the neighborhoods in which they seek to operate to be unaware of the social context of their arrival. Our society's academic institutions have not generally prioritized sharing meaningful knowledge about the making of modern cities, to say nothing of the intentional barriers to economic vibrancy placed in front of some communities motivated by racial discrimination or other factors. Brewery ownership does not reflect the diversity of many of our neighborhoods. In a demographic audit of brewery owners done by the Brewer's Association in 2019, approximately six percent identified themselves as people of color (Watson, 2021).

This chapter helps explore the foundations of the economic roadblocks to progress in diverse neighborhoods as context for understanding two key challenges. First, these barriers have made it more difficult for diverse operators to participate in the craft beer industry. Some of the most recognizable current and former craft brands got their start with capital from family and friends – networks frequently not harmed by the policies of the past. This is not the fault of those brands, and we ought not get bogged down in a blame game, but rather seek to understand the impediments to inclusion which intentional historical discrimination has caused. A second key challenge is in the neighborhoods that have often become ideal candidates for fledgling brewery operations. The barriers that have impacted access to capital have also hard-wired a lack of economic mobility in many of these same, often racially diverse neighborhoods. This second challenge, however, is more about the opportunity to leverage the assets that these neighborhoods have in culture and community and in many cases industrious microenterprise and to ensure greater inclusion extends to partnerships forged within these new communities.

Barriers to inclusive economic growth

The economic hardships caused by COVID-19 brought significant lessons, specifically to the Community Development Finance Institution (CDFI)

DOI: 10.4324/9781003371564-9

industry, community lenders and the economic development community. Racial wealth gap issues rooted in our economic systems became even more apparent and clear as capital deployment (including PPP and other stimulus-related funds) lagged within communities of color. Business owners of color have unequal access to credit due to antiquated and exclusionary underwriting, a broken capital delivery system, and a limited and predatory product set. For example, the Federal Reserve Small Business Credit Survey revealed that non-Hispanic Black, Latino, and Asian applicants received a third less credit than sought as compared to the national average (Weirsch et al., 2021). Business owners of color have trouble securing capital due to:

- Persistent discrimination
- Fear and reality of rejection
- Lower levels of wealth due to systemic racism and disenfranchisement
- Experience, location, and industry sectors

We recognize that we have a core systemic problem. A tiny fraction of mainstream capital is moving into community finance. While the impact market remains a small portion of overall capital markets, it is evolving despite the community and economic development sector's inability to provide consistent scalable opportunities to invest.

One issue is that these Community Intermediaries, of which CDFIs are an example, are ill-equipped due to the following reasons:

- Fragmented on-the-ground demand in communities of color makes it challenging to innovate and scale enough to connect with capital sources
- Inability of current set of intermediaries, mostly CDFIs, to deploy capital with both financial and social returns at scale
- Lack of intermediaries focused in communities of color who can provide sophisticated financial services with a level of expertise to which mainstream markets are accustomed and who can adequately screen and monitor investments
- Mainstream investors increasingly want to deploy capital at scale into communities, while maintaining geographic and portfolio diversification, but scale and diversification does not currently exist

According to Small Business Surveys of 2020 and 2021, CDFIs were the most impactful lenders in supporting small businesses through the pandemic (Weirsch et al., 2021). However, they remain sub-scale relative to the overall market due to a lack of product diversity, balance sheet constraints and inefficiencies and technological limitations in operations. Therefore, CDFIs can better scale their impact if equipped with new products and technology that can support them in deploying capital at scale.

Black, Indigenous, People of Color (BIPOC) business owner challenges

Rising inequality has been manifesting in ways that fracture communities and strain the fabric of society. Underinvested communities face vulnerabilities across healthcare, education, housing, food, and at the core – equality of opportunity. According to the US Census, in 2020, approximately 37.2 million people lived in poverty, representing a poverty rate of 11.4%; the Black population had the highest poverty rate among major racial groups (19.5%) and the Hispanic population had a poverty rate of 17.0%. The median wealth of the typical White family is 8× that of the typical Black family and 5× that of the typical Hispanic family. Whether examined by income or wealth, the situation is the same: the gap to achieving healthy and opportunity-filled communities is widening, especially in communities of color.

A leading contributor to this economic inequity is a lack of access to capital and credit. The US Department of Commerce has studied this pattern of lack of access for many years. One study found that minority firms received lower loan amounts even when controlled for firm size as compared to their non-minority counterparts (Fairlie & Robb, 2010). Another study found that "African American-owned businesses were more likely to have a loan application denied, even after controlling for differences in creditworthiness, and that African Americans paid a higher interest rate on loans obtained" (Fairlie & Robb, 2010, p. 21). In a recent analysis of financing sought during the pandemic, Black-owned firms received 24% of the financing they sought, compared with 48% for White-owned firms (Battisto et al., 2022). These inequities may be due to antiquated and exclusionary underwriting, a broken capital delivery system, and limited and predatory products.

Furthermore, the organizations traditionally relied upon to address systemic poverty – CDFIs – are themselves facing uncertain business models that threaten their long-term sustainability and efficacy. The $17 trillion in US assets under management using environmental social and governance screens and the 40 trillion dollars in wealth that is expected to be transferred to the next generation could help, but current economic structures do not facilitate investments in true community impact. Less than 1% of these funds are managed by CDFIs. If they were able to access these pools of capital, CDFIs could improve their liquidity and scale their impact. However, CDFIs struggle to tap these capital markets because existing intermediaries are ill-equipped to raise and deploy capital at the necessary scale to attract institutional investors.

While these challenges are by no means exclusive to would-be brewery owners of color, the economic challenges have deep roots in the nation's history that have intensified the depth of the impact for some groups. Understanding this in a more fundamental way is important to addressing its impacts on inclusion in craft beer and is explored further in the next section.

Land use, local government and equity

The story of craft breweries across the United States in the early to mid-2000s has been a mixed one for a variety of reasons. In the context of diverse communities, a complex set of policy and economic factors have shaped the contours of this story. As a threshold matter, understanding which locations lend themselves to craft and nano brewery operations helps lay the groundwork for a more complicated picture of both tremendous opportunity and, in some cases, significant challenges.

To stand up a small operation with limited capital, selecting locations that have inexpensive leases and where neighborhood resistance is minimal have been important considerations for some start-up breweries. From a land use perspective, in many communities this means considering sites in or near industrial areas or in economically depressed communities with relatively low lease rates. These areas tend to have fewer formal community structures for opposition, less political clout, and greater flexibility for use of sites. See Chapter 5 for more on gentrification issues.

Although research suggests that craft breweries more frequently follow neighborhood change than drive it (Reid, 2018; Walker & Miller, 2018), a further look reveals this may depend in part on when one starts the clock, so to speak. For example, in San Diego's North Park neighborhood a careful examination reveals that there are breweries such as Mike Hess Brewing that opened in the early stages of neighborhood change and could be seen as drivers – or at least an early catalyst – to that change. Conversely, newer entrants (relative to Hess) to the same neighborhood such as North Park Beer, Fall Brewing, and Rouleur Brewing may be seen either as entering a community already experiencing investment-related upward pressure or simply part of a longer process of neighborhood change. For example, the buildings where the newer breweries opened were locations of substantial investment and could have attracted subsequent market participants.

In most American cities the most attractive places for these free-spirited start-ups also tend to be the most diverse neighborhoods in those cities. In the early part of the 20th century, a mixture of racially restrictive covenants and racially discriminatory lending practices converged to depress values and concentrate people of color in certain parts of most cities. Rothstein lays out in painstaking detail the ways that land use policy acted to concentrate communities of color and economic depression in American cities (Rothstein, 2018). In addition to the restrictive covenants and redlining[1] lending practices, several areas surrounding cities in California, New York, and elsewhere went a step further and created inexpensive suburban neighborhoods available only to White residents, further concentrating those with lower incomes in these urban and near-industrial areas. As a result of the decades of disinvestment, these same neighborhoods became the inexpensive fertile ground from which the modern craft beer resurgence has sprouted.

While the upsides to siting breweries in these distressed or "emerging" neighborhoods are well-documented (see Chapter 2 for an in-depth look), there are also important caveats when it comes to considering the equity impacts of breweries. Considerable work has been done to evaluate the degree of displacement,[2] sometimes referred to as gentrification. Gibbons and Barton laid out several compelling cases that one of the primary harms to be accounted for is not displacement but rather the elimination of a sense of belonging (Gibbons & Barton, 2016). The question becomes not just whether a person or ethnic group that has considered a community to be its home is technically forced to move due to rising costs brought on by increased economic activity. Rather, a key question of equity is whether these same people feel marginalized or less welcome in the same neighborhood as a result of the changes to cultural and social fabric.

A substantial contribution to the academic literature in this area has been made by Chapman and Brunsma (2020) in their chapter *Beer and Racism: How Beer Became White, Why it Matters and The Movements to Change It*. Frequently, the mere inclusion of a charged term like racism shuts down otherwise healthy and productive discussion. What we learn from their work is that the complexity of racial impacts on the world of independent craft beer ought not be subject to a reductive and binary argument about personalized animus. The discussion of racism in craft beer is rarely truly about whether an individual owner, beertender or investor harbors racist attitudes towards potential customers. Indeed, it is a more reasonable expectation that diverse patrons or participants and their dollars would be welcomed expansions to a brewery's client base. Much more relevant to a conversation about racism in this context, and adeptly addressed in great detail within *Beer and Racism*, is the more complex set of social and economic factors that are not about current blame, but about future progress. The purpose of this chapter is not to replicate this thoughtful academic research and analysis. Rather, we seek here to draw the connections between this clarifying work that contextualizes the evolution of a complicated sociological phenomenon and the practical manifestation of that phenomenon in the context of land use and neighborhoods.

This chapter provided insight into the existing barriers to inclusion for diverse would-be entrants to the industry and the strained evolution of land use policy that has limited the breadth and depth of a potential customer base and source of industry partners. We end with some tips for real-world implementation to move in a more diverse, equitable direction for all craft beer owners, brewers and consumers.

Tips for the practitioner

While there are a number of ways to shape the growth of the industry in cities, for planners, community leaders, craft brewers/investors and economic development professionals, certain steps can help maximize an equitable approach to attracting and opening craft breweries.

Tip #1: Ensure participatory and inclusive land use changes

One thing we have learned in a variety of local settings is that government and academic institutions can fail communities by arriving with a paternalistic approach to what the entities believe will be good for the community. Incorporating specific approval requirements to engage neighborhoods prior to securing building permits is a straightforward way to improve the interaction between the potential new neighbor and the community it is entering. However, it need not be a requirement that the community approve every aspect of the design and product plans. Institutions can and should provide guidance for authentic engagement that is participatory, in languages understood in the community, and ensures that the potential owners have attempted to understand and blend with the identities shared by the existing residents and other small businesses. This does not mean that a new brewery need lose its own identity, of course. Merely that an earnest attempt to contextualize the operation and embrace the fabric of the neighborhood as it is at the time can have dramatic positive impacts for inclusion.

Tip #2: Engage and support the neighborhood

The mantra of shopping local has taken hold in many communities. This concept can and should be extended to the practice of hiring. From grassroots flier campaigns to working with local workforce agencies and community colleges, both financial institutions and would-be brewery operators have plenty of vehicles for seeking to employ people who are part of the community in which they propose to operate. In addition, many neighborhoods have built-in ecosystems for sourcing art or complementary goods for the brewery from within. One example of this is Border X Brewing in the Barrio Logan neighborhood of San Diego. And the advent of Microenterprise Home Kitchen Ordinances that allow residents to monetize their home kitchens which can have profound impacts for sourcing locally and creating a deeper sense of inclusion within the community.

Tip #3: Plan, track and report on results

Local governments are the primary entity capable of requiring some level of tracking as to the attempts made to be inclusive as breweries seek new opportunities. Requiring that final permit approvals demonstrate that attempts were made – and the results of those attempts – can further enhance the depth of work done prior to establishing a new location in diverse communities. Another opportunity lies with the state entity responsible for licensing the sale of alcoholic beverages. These entities need to take care to not become overly burdensome for breweries attempting to achieve their primary mission – the production and sale of a quality product – establishing simple guideposts is attainable. For example, as part of an annual process a brewery could be required to document efforts it has made in a one-page form related to collaboration with the community in which it operates. Additionally, the Brewers Association lays out in its Diversity Best Practices Playlist a number of thoughtful ways a new brewery can choose to self-assess on specific issues of diversity and inclusion (Jackson-Beckham, 2019). These include things like setting goals for inclusive hiring and recruitment, events, and geographic reach – all significant in building a space that is connected to the community in which it operates.

The world of local, independent breweries and the people they serve is one filled with upsides for communities. The term "craft" as applied to beer has faced a range of definitional and social challenges and disputes about what it means and what it applies to. However, there is little doubt that the spirit of hard work, creativity, sacrifice and independence that has defined the industry's smallest brewers is alive and well. As the industry continues to mature and the government and civic structures that support it evolve, the need to support a holistic and inclusive approach to breweries is expanding.

Notes

1 See Mapping Inequality: Redlining in New Deal America (https://dsl.richmond.edu/panorama/redlining/#loc=5/39.1/-94.58) for more information.
2 See Urban Displacement Project (www.urbandisplacement.org/) for more information.

7 Craft Breweries and Crime

Not All Alcohol Establishments Are Created Equally

Julie Wartell

Introduction

The number of craft breweries has skyrocketed over the last 20 years. This growth has sparked questions about their effects on the neighborhoods in which they are located and those nearby. Research shows many positive changes (as discussed in several other chapters). One aspect of this growth that has only begun to be examined is the effect breweries have on neighborhood crime and disorder. There has been a large amount of research over the years connecting alcohol and bars with crime and disorder problems (Madensen & Eck, 2008; Sherman et al., 1992; Quigley et al., 2003; Roncek & Maier, 1991; Gruenewald, 2007; Scott & Dedel, 2006). When examining why bars are considered "risky facilities" – types of places where a small number of locations account for a large percentage of the crime (Eck et al., 2007), one should consider that not all bars are equal in terms of generating a higher-than-average amount of crime. The growth of craft breweries over the last 20 years provides an opportunity to examine if breweries differ from typical bars and why. This chapter will include background research on bar-related crime, research on breweries and crime, a discussion about what factors are likely contributing to lower incidents of crime at breweries, and how breweries are applying the concept of situational crime prevention.

Crime Research: Bars Versus Breweries

For this chapter, I will be discussing crime and disorder problems that have been uniquely associated with alcohol establishments such as bars, taverns, pubs, and so on. I will not address crimes within these places that also are common to other types of businesses (such as burglary, theft, and forgery). Research on alcohol establishments and crime will be discussed with reference to routine activity theory (Cohen & Felson, 1979), rational choice theory (Cornish & Clarke, 1986), crime generators and attractors (Brantingham & Brantingham, 1995), and situational crime prevention (Clarke, 1980, 1995).

DOI: 10.4324/9781003371564-10

Bars are known to be "crime generators" – places that attract a lot of people for reasons not related to crime. Although some bars can also be considered "crime attractors" – places that provide a great deal of opportunity for crime and disorderly behavior. This opportunity is due to having many suitable crime targets (drunk individuals) coming together (in or just outside a bar) with a lack of capable guardianship (such as bartenders or other place managers) – the premise of routine activity theory. We also know that crime concentrates around bars, especially with lower alcohol prices (Madensen & Eck, 2008; Sherman et al., 1992; Quigley et al., 2003). Not all bars generate crime problems equally (Eck et al., 2007). In a study in Milwaukee, Sherman et al. (1992) found that "slightly over 15 percent of all taverns were found to produce consistently over half of all tavern crime."

Research has shown that bar-focused problems relate to neighborhood setting, patrons, type of bar, and management practices (Roncek & Maier, 1991; Gruenewald, 2007; Madensen & Eck, 2008; Lipton et al., 2013). Other studies have found that land use (Twinam, 2017), density of outlets (Toomey et al., 2012; Livingston, 2011; Campbell et al., 2009), and social organization (Pridemore & Grubesic, 2012) matter for explaining the amount of crime relating to bars.

Very little has been written about breweries as a specific type of alcohol establishment regarding crime. The first study to examine this issue found that the opening of a craft brewery does not have a significant effect on crime in the immediate area around its location (Nilsson et al., 2020). A study done in Louisville, Kentucky, looked at "alternative gentrification" indicators (with craft breweries being one) and found that their presence was correlated with a decrease in robberies (Noonan, 2017). In an unpublished study examining bars versus breweries in Portland, Oregon, I found that bars with liquor had more than three times the number of police calls than breweries (Wartell, 2016). Another way of examining the issue is through "Last Drink" survey data. An analysis done a few years ago analyzing this data for a southern California county found that a small number of locations accounted for many mentions (Wartell, 2017). Of the 647 people who named an establishment as the place of last drink, one location accounted for 11% of all mentions. One brewery was mentioned once and one brewpub four times, but no breweries were in the top 20 (with 7 or more mentions).

Several studies have focused on reducing or preventing crime problems in and around bars, but to date, none have examined breweries. One of the leading approaches to reducing crime is situational crime prevention (SCP), which "seeks to reduce opportunities for specific categories of crime by increasing the associated risks and difficulties and reducing the rewards" (Clarke, 1995, p. 91). The SCP classification system includes five categories (increase the effort, increase the risks, reduce the rewards, reduce provocations, and remove excuses) along with five techniques for each (Cornish & Clarke, 2003). The researchers who have studied bar-related crime have found that applying SCP can work. Madensen and Eck (2008) found that good place management related to less violence. In a study in Bogota, Columbia, researchers learned that bartenders, one type of place manager, can play a role in curbing consumption and promoting good behavior (Ham et al., 2022). Another study in Australia that examined the security environment at nightclub entrances found that they can "prompt, pressure, permit and provoke anti-social behaviour by creating disputes, frustrations and stresses" (Cozens & Grieve, 2014, p. 66). In Graham and Homel's book (2008), several chapters are devoted to discussing the environment and guardianship of bars as well as two chapters discussing prevention techniques grounded in routine activity and rational choice theories as well as SCP.

Craft Brewery Characteristics

A core thesis of this chapter is that craft breweries are different from bars both qualitatively and quantitatively. The following section outlines the characteristics that make craft breweries different from many bars.

1. Type of Patrons. Walk into most breweries and you will find families, from babies through elderly. You will also find dogs (and once in a brewery in Pennsylvania, a woman had her pet hamster!). Although this is not universally true for all breweries, there are websites devoted to which craft breweries are baby-, kid-, and dog-friendly.
2. Surrounding Environment. Many breweries consider themselves a community-gathering spot for friends, neighbors, strangers, and families to enjoy a beer. There are often board games, no TVs, and big community tables. Some have taken historic buildings and/or integrated local themes. One study in Montana found that "craft breweries play a significant role in contemporary place-making" (Fletchall, 2016). Read more about breweries and their environment in Chapter 2.
3. Surrounding land use. As discussed in several other chapters, many craft breweries are in office parks or out-of-the-way warehouse locations. While clusters of breweries are conducive to brewery districts and beer tourism, people who are looking for drunken bar-hopping in an entertainment district will not usually find a craft brewery.
4. Earlier closing time. Most breweries are not open as late as bars. Some people say nothing good happens after midnight; fortunately, most breweries do not have to worry. This also relates to the clientele – if you have families, they are more likely to be going home earlier.
5. No liquor/spirits. Craft breweries do not usually sell liquor. Of the ones that do, they are more likely brewpubs that include restaurants and are also more family-oriented. Drinkers who are looking to "do shots" will need to look elsewhere.

6. Higher prices. Due to the higher costs of making craft beer, breweries tend to charge more for a pint than a typical bar. People are willing to pay these higher prices, often because they are only having one or two beers during a visit.

Situational Crime Prevention and Breweries

In addition to these characteristics, what further explanations could exist for why breweries do not typically have the same amount of crime problems as other alcohol establishments? I suggest it is because they are applying situational crime prevention. Because crime and disorder associated with alcohol establishments relate to offender behavior, place management, and other environmental factors as described earlier, these types of locations are conducive to a situational crime prevention approach. Graham, a Canadian researcher from the Center for Addiction even created a framework to apply SCP to prevent alcohol-related violence as seen in Figure 7.1 (2009).

An example of a city considering these issues comes from Orlando, Florida, and the Broken Cauldron Brewing plans. The Orlando Police Department reviewed the plans as part of the Conditional Use Permit (CUP) using Crime Prevention through Environmental Design principles, which overlap SCP relating to natural surveillance, access control, territorial reinforcement, and target hardening.[1] Based on the SCP table of 25 techniques, this final section will describe how craft breweries are currently applying them (without knowing they are following crime prevention theories) or could apply many of them.[2]

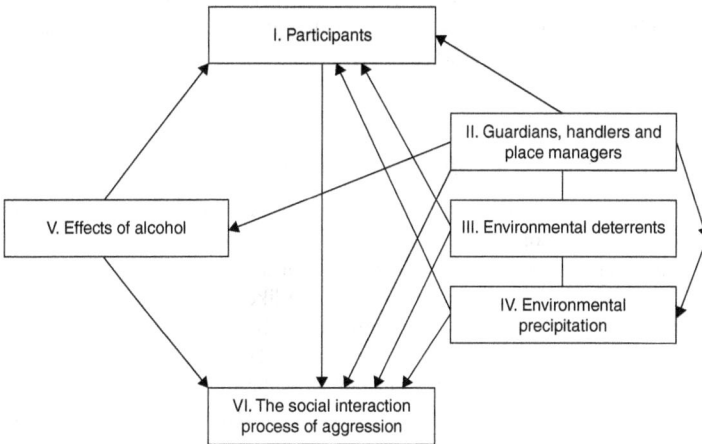

Figure 7.1 A situational crime prevention model for preventing alcohol-related violence.

CATEGORY 1 – Increase the Effort: make it more difficult to commit the crime

Target hardening is the idea of making targets of theft or vandalism more difficult. While these are not typically the types of crimes that are discussed when talking about alcohol establishments and crime, logo glass theft and keg theft do often occur. Some of the prevention techniques have been security tags with ink-exploding devices, alarms in the glasses, and deposits, but unfortunately, deposits have not prevented the keg theft problem as much as breweries would like.[3] Prevention measures such as alarms and deposits also relate to *screening exits*, which ensures that people are not stealing anything or leaving without paying.

Controlling access to facilities is defined as keeping people out of places where they do not have the right to be in. For alcohol establishments, the most common technique is to ask for identification of drinking age. But importantly, and this relates to place management practices, it is also about refusing entry or service to people who are already intoxicated.

Deflecting offenders includes keeping rivals or potential combatants away from one another. There was a brewery in San Diego's east county (home to several biker gangs) that had a sign about not wearing gang colors, and a bar in Taylor, Michigan, had a similar sign. The bar's owner noted, "There's a lot of bikers in this area, and that's just to keep the biker gangs (from) getting into it with each other" (USA Today, 2014).

The last technique in this category, *control tools/weapons*, started way back in the Wild West when gun fights occurred in the bars. In modern times, there are laws about not bringing in guns or weapons to alcohol establishments, but bars in the UK have even changed their glassware to make them harder to break and thus use as a weapon.[4]

CATEGORY 2 – Increase the Risks: make it likelier for the offender to get caught

Extending guardianship means having the presence of people beyond employees or official security. One way that breweries have extended guardianship is through their welcoming of families. Common sense says that the more people there are who are not likely to be involved in crime, the better. When Insight Brewing from Minneapolis, Minnesota, was in planning, the Inspector's Report noted, "Because this warehouse has been vacant for several years, Insight feels their presence at this location will help deter criminal activity" (Minnesota Department of Agriculture, undated).

Assisting natural surveillance is accomplished through allowing the place to be seen by more people. When there is an ability to observe the entire area, it reduces the likelihood of customers getting away with bad behavior. This is done at breweries via open spaces, lighting, and even being open early for coffee, which encourages a constant flow of people throughout the day.

Reducing anonymity increases the number of people who are known to the employees and place managers. Some breweries allow regulars to have their own mugs, and the integration in the neighborhoods encourages more customers and employees to know one another. Another strategy bars and breweries are using to reduce sexual assault is providing a code word that allows a woman to secretly identify a person to a bartender who will then in turn help the woman get away from them.

Using place managers is the idea that someone there is responsible for the overall activities at the place. An aspect of many craft breweries is that the owner(s) and/or brewer(s) are often on-site and serve this role. The more people who care about the place and can take action, the better to control bad behavior.

Strengthening formal surveillance includes increasing the number of security staff and/or devices that can observe problem behavior. In Broken Cauldron Brewing's CUP, it noted, "A uniformed security guard should be hired to continually patrol the construction site during the hours when construction work has ceased" (Broken Cauldron, 2015).

CATEGORY 3 – Reduce the Rewards: *affect the benefits received by committing the crime*

These benefits or rewards might be financial, power. The only technique within this category that applies is *denying benefits*. Controlling how much alcohol people consume will reduce their opportunity to get drunk and exert power or worse attacking or fighting.

CATEGORY 4 – Reduce Provocations: *focus on situational factors that precipitate crime*

Reducing frustrations and stress eases everyone, but people at risk of offending may act out on their frustrations in a more troublesome way. Partially due to building codes and regulations, as well as atmosphere, craft breweries often have smaller numbers of people in their tasting rooms than you'd expect at a typical bar. Additionally, clear signage and proper queues assist with this.

Neutralizing peer pressure minimizes the one-upped-ness that often occurs in alcohol establishments. While some breweries offer happy hours for discounts on beers, most breweries do not serve spirits or foster a culture of drinking to excess with promotions such as $1 shots or 2-for-1 drinks.

Once again, the atmosphere of families and mellow community-gathering location are not conducive to peer-pressure drinking.

CATEGORY 5 – Remove Excuses: ensure that offenders cannot rationalize their conduct

Setting rules ensures that people are aware of expected conduct. While having families at craft breweries has many positive outcomes for crime prevention, some breweries have found that misbehaving children are causing problems. Some breweries have moved to not allowing kids after a certain time such as 8pm.

Posting instructions follows setting rules and letting everyone know those rules in an easy-to-read manner. This has included setting limits on the number of beers, especially higher alcohol ones. Rules relating to children and dogs include signs about their behavior as well as the behavior of the parents.

Alerting conscience attempts to cause people to think twice before committing the crime or causing the problem. Breweries use signage to alert patrons that people outside the establishment are affected. For instance, the sign at Left Field Brewery in Toronto, Canada, states, "please respect our neighbours and keep noise and litter to a minimum."

Assisting compliance helps give people an alternative. Many breweries offer "taster" size glasses of their beers, and higher alcohol beers are only served in smaller size glasses (e.g., 10 oz instead of 16 oz). In this regard, breweries are reducing the opportunity to get drunk. As mentioned earlier, some also have a limit on how many of these higher alcohol beers you are allowed to drink. Many brewery festivals provide cheap or free tickets for designated drivers to encourage people not to drink and drive. The example of the higher alcohol beer limits also relates to the last technique of *controlling drugs and alcohol.*

As we've seen in this chapter, the relatively new and growing craft brewery industry has not been shown to generate crime as bars have in the past, and there are many characteristics of craft breweries that could explain why this is the case. However, there have been very few studies especially in the peer-reviewed literature. Further research is needed on which of these factors and characteristics that are more prevalent in craft breweries than bars are likely related to lower crime and quality-of-life issues as well as which situational crime prevention strategies are most effective in maintaining lower crime and disorder at craft breweries.

Notes

1 Entire plan can be found at www.cityoforlando.net/greenworks/wp-content/uploads/sites/27/2015/07/MPBStaffReport2015-07_CUP2015-00008.pdf.

2 The full table and more information on each of the techniques can be found on the Center for Problem-Oriented Policing's website.

3 See www.dailymail.co.uk/sciencetech/article-2360155/Pubs-desperate-stop-customers-stealing-glasses-fit-INK-EXPLODING-security-tags.html, www.theguardian.com/world/2018/mar/15/belgian-bars-put-the-boot-into-tourists-who-steal-beer-glasses, and www.brewersassociation.org/brewing-industry-updates/steel-not-steal-keg-loss-continues-industry-problem/.

4 See www.independent.co.uk/news/tougher-glasses-to-cut-pub-violence-1256380.html.

8 Craft Breweries and Sustainability

Civic Solutions Through Leadership and Innovation

Joseph LeRoy

Introduction – The Concept of Sustainability

Younger generations continue to expand their growing impact on the greater economy and the markets within it, "committed to making choices that align with their values" (Petro, 2022). Three fourths of Gen Z state that sustainability is more important than a product's brand name when making purchase decisions. They are not alone. Today, nearly 90% of Gen X consumers said that they would be willing to spend 10% extra or more for sustainable products, compared to just over 34% two years ago. In fact, consumers across the board have shown a rising willingness to pay an additional 10% for sustainable products (First Insight, 2021). When considering craft beer drinkers and their interest in premium products, it comes as no surprise that they are more aware of their purchasing behavior and how it affects the environment and are willing to pay more for sustainably produced beer (Carley & Yahng, 2018).

To better understand how sustainability initiatives impact the brewing industry, it is important to establish a basic understanding of the movement's foundations. While environmentalists have long debated measures of and frameworks for sustainability, John Elkington has been largely credited as one of the founding authorities of the modern understanding of corporate responsibility and sustainable business (A Simple Explanation). Elkington coined the term "Triple Bottom Line" (TBL) in 1994 (Elkington, 2013), which includes three core dimensions, or bottom lines, which corporations could use to transform their financially focused accounting systems to analyze more than just their monetary impact (Slaper & Hall, 2011). Elkington used TBL to illustrate the connections between the social, environmental, and economic impacts that an organization has upon the world it operates within. He later expanded it into the concept of the Three P's: People, Planet, and Profit.

- **People (Social Bottom Line):** How is an organization impacting its stakeholders? Beyond investors, this includes employees, families of those employees, customers they serve, suppliers they partner with, and the greater communities they exist within.

DOI: 10.4324/9781003371564-11

- **Planet (Environmental Bottom Line):** How is the organization impacting the planet? This concept covers a variety of considerations, from limiting natural resource consumption to mitigating waste to landfill to reducing the organization's carbon footprint.
- **Profit (Economic Bottom Line):** How is the organization impacting its economy? This pillar goes beyond profits and losses and includes the generation of innovation, employment opportunities, local taxes, and wealth creation.

Elkington's framework will be used as a lens to illustrate the concept of corporate sustainability in the brewing industry.

Each of these core dimensions are interconnected. For example, economic profit can extend beyond the financial success of the organization, recognizing the "profit" for the local community when job opportunities are created. Environmental success can positively impact the social bottom line, as cleaner air and water results in a healthier population. Social success through happy and healthy employees who provide safe environments for their families will ultimately help grow a greater community, with better businesses and a better supply chain, benefiting the economic bottom line. This framework provides corporate leadership the opportunity to rethink capitalism with long-term strategic success in mind.

Triple Bottom Brewing has literally made a name for themselves by embodying this concept as a founding principle. Championing "Beer, People, and Planet," they recognize that producing beer allows the company to make a positive impact (Triple Bottom Brewing, n.d.). They've partnered with local nonprofits to recruit candidates who've experienced homelessness or incarceration, providing employment and growth opportunities for their immediate community (Kovach, 2020). They have documented their water, electricity, and gas consumption since inception, sourcing all electricity from wind-generated power sources within the state and connecting with local agricultural partners that receive their spent grain waste (Morales, 2022). Triple Bottom has even gone through the arduous process of becoming a Certified B Corp through B Lab.[1] In doing so, Triple Bottom has joined Allagash, Brewery Vivant, New Belgium, and other industry leaders (Eco-Friendly Beer Drinker, 2020).

Certification as a B Corp starts with an assessment of impact, measuring practices, and outputs across governance, workers, community, the environment, and customers. Then, the assessment is benchmarked against other assessed businesses. It is evaluated, verified via documentation (Bcorporation.net., 2023), and returned to the applicant. If the threshold for qualification is met, the information is published by B Lab as part of their transparency directive. The process is long, intensive, and costly but clearly illustrates how businesses that achieve the status are differentiating themselves by upholding to a higher set of standards (Toth, 2020, p. 77). It also requires recertification every three years, requiring continuous improvement. This differentiation highlights the importance of gathering information, benchmarking, and communicating internally and externally.

Another example of certifying sustainability efforts is 1% For the Planet. A "global movement inspiring businesses and individuals to support environmental solutions," members of this nonprofit organization donate at least 1% of their annual sales to approved environmental partners. Pure Project Brewing, since its opening in 2016, has made partnering with nonprofits a core principle (Pure Project, 2022). As a certified member of 1% For the Planet, the San Diego brewery supports causes that impact the core focuses of their sustainability framework as outlined by Environmental and Community Impact Manager Cassie Dexter Torti: education, regeneration, and legislation (Wartell and Vasquez, Pure). Internally, the business educates and certifies employees through the eight nonprofits they focus upon. Externally, they market and host events that highlight environmental efforts of partnered nonprofits. Beyond their commitment to donations, they also hold themselves to the high standards of the Climate Neutral organization, certifying since 2019 that their activities result in no net effect on the climate system, meeting standards for measuring, offsetting, and reducing greenhouse gas emissions (Climate Neutral, 2022). Lastly, they are Certified Plastic Neutral, committing their products to a neutralized plastic footprint and contributing to the collection and recycling of an equivalent amount of plastic used in their products and packaging on a yearly basis (Plastic Bank, 2022). These certifications communicate the efforts that organizations are making toward sustainability, providing metrics for measuring impact and improving the triple bottom line.

Sustainability Metrics

Moving a business toward greater sustainability requires consistent performance assessment and reporting of environmental, societal, and economic indicators (Tokos et al., 2012). Breweries operate with very complex mechanical systems that rely upon large volumes of regularly varied inputs. A robust supply chain, ingredients, energy, water, and labor are all necessary to produce beer. To assess a brewery's impact and support effective decision making, sustainable development indicators must be measured not just periodically but also in a live environment over a sustained period, allowing for comparisons and benchmarking with other businesses (Singh et al., 2009; Jasch, 2000).

Luckily, there are now resources to support small- and medium-sized breweries in navigating the complexities of sustainability metrics and data tracking. The Brewer's Association has produced manuals addressing energy usage, greenhouse gas reduction, water consumption, solid and water waste, and sustainable facility design (Brewers Association). They've also developed sustainability benchmarking templates that allow smaller breweries to take advantage of the experience of their peers, standardizing data sets and making comparisons between businesses easier.

These resources help promote a culture of awareness, transparency, and sustainability that has become a part of the very fabric of the craft beer industry. Many breweries have published sustainability reports on their websites, inviting the public to audit their sustainability efforts.

An early adopter and market leader in sustainability, Brewery Vivant has made the triple bottom line a core value since inception (Wartell and Vasquez, Vivant). Owner and president Kris Spaulding previously worked in the sustainability business unit of Herman Miller, a Michigan furniture manufacturer. When she and her husband opened their own brewery, she combined her passion, her degree in Environmental Policy and Behavior, and her MBA to develop a business plan that would uphold those ideals from the onset. Founded in 2010 in Grand Rapids, Michigan, Brewery Vivant quickly began collecting accolades. In 2012, they became the first ever LEED-certified production brewery in the United States (Newell, 2012). The designation is bestowed by the US Green Building Council, certifying that the facility itself is energy efficient, conserves water, and reduces greenhouse gas emissions. The brewery is housed within an 80-year-old building, while the brewpub is built within a 1948 chapel that was renovated following the strict Historic Preservation standards, preserving the historic value of the building (Brewery Vivant, 2022).

Brewery Vivant has also made assessment and reporting a priority, publishing sustainability reports every year since 2011. These publications outline their goals and where they stand in relation to them and communicate their values to their stakeholders. They are also a staple of B Corp businesses, a certification the brewery achieved in 2014 (Wells). In particular, the reports showcase the efforts to positively impact the people and community they interact with. In their 2021 report, they highlight that over 75% of all purchases were made in Michigan, and over 60% of food was produced using Michigan ingredients. 1% of all sales went to local charities, and voluntary turnover of staff was almost 50% lower than industry standards. They also outline desired outcomes of their DEIJA (diversity, equity, inclusion, justice, accessibility) committee. These efforts, along with their ongoing employee education, help every member of the organization embody their TBL (Wartell and Vasquez, Vivant).

> Something that we have done from the beginning, and I think it's important . . . [is] educating our staff on 'What does it mean . . .'? 'What is all of this,' 'why does it matter to them and the company'.
>
> (Kris Spaulding)

Beer is Resource Intensive

The production of beer is an incredibly resource-intensive process (Olajire, 2020). Breweries must source ingredients that demand agricultural land and water use. Those ingredients must be transported and delivered. Once onsite, those ingredients must be processed with energy, water, and human labor to produce a final product. Then, those products must be packaged and distributed to the marketplace. The efficiency of the energy and water systems, packaging equipment, labor force, and supply chain partners all directly influence how the brewery impacts the TBL. Measuring, monitoring, and improving these impacts are equally demanding.

Ingredients

When considering the agricultural nature of beer, how ingredients are grown, harvested, processed, and delivered, the sourcing of ingredients becomes an important consideration for breweries hoping to understand and control their environmental impact. In the modern marketplace, consumers and conscious business managers want to understand how a product has been produced (Cheung, 2019). A brewery's supply chain can reflect how seriously they are taking their sustainability efforts. Balancing cost, purchasing power, and transportation, a brewery can highlight their use of local, organic, or consciously grown ingredients (Grunde et al., 2014). They can consider the impact of travel distances and what that means for the environment. They can design their workflows to better utilize and process their ingredients to minimize waste.

Water

National and global water challenges are becoming more problematic as climate change continues to put pressure on already strained resources (Klobucista and Robinson, 2021). Demand for water in the United States has more than tripled between 1950 and 2000 and continues to grow to this day (Brewer's Association). The Brewers Association (BA) took an official position on water as part of their greater effort to "promote and protect American craft brewers, their beers, and the community of brewing enthusiasts." The position statement reads: *Water is the primary ingredient in beer. The BA recognizes that safe, clean, affordable, and readily available water is an essential resource to member breweries and that access to water is a basic human right. The BA supports actively protecting and conserving America's water resources, which are critical to the long-term vitality of craft brewers and our supplier partners as well as the health and safety of every community* (Skypeck, 2020, p. 44). By taking this position, the BA has codified its efforts in shepherding the industry toward greater sustainability.

Water is arguably the single most important ingredient in beer, making up over 90% of the final product. Water supplies impact breweries at nearly every level of production. Agricultural suppliers require huge volumes of water to grow the hops, barley, wheat, and other ingredients. Droughts are becoming more severe, intense, and widespread, heavily impacting many of the regions that have historically provided the core ingredients in beer (Patel and Tierney, 2022). The brewing process itself is also water intensive, using on average seven gallons for every gallon of beer produced. Breweries have begun to address their role in finding more sustainable solutions for how they utilize and conserve water. From 2015 to 2020, total water used by breweries participating in the Beverage Industry Environmental Roundtable (BIER) decreased by over 12 billion gallons, an 11% decrease (Beverage Industry Environmental Roundtable, 2022). While many of the participating members of BIER enjoy scales of economy not possible for smaller breweries, there are best practices that are making a difference across the entire industry.

The first step, as with nearly any sustainability initiative, is comprehensive monitoring and self-analysis. By understanding what is coming into and leaving the business along with the associated costs, a brewery's inefficiencies, defective equipment, and poor processes can be improved. Some best practices that have come from the active monitoring of water usage are adjusting flow, adjusting current equipment, changing to new equipment, reusing or recycling water, and shifting to a low-water or waterless process (Brewers Association).

Energy

Energy consumption is another major consideration for breweries. There are typically two forms of energy utilized by breweries: thermal energy, such as fossil fuel and natural gas, and electricity. Brewing tends to consume the greatest volume of thermal energy, with packaging, utilities and space heating contributing as well. Electrical costs also include major contributors such as refrigeration, packaging, and lighting (Brewers Association). Despite an average brewery using 70% of its energy consumption on thermal applications, these fossil fuel inputs typically amount to only 30% of the total energy cost, making the reduction of electricity use a significant financial incentive (Pullman et al., 2015).

As with any resource, the first step in managing energy consumption is data collection and self-monitoring. Using the growing body of work provided by organizations such as the BA, state industry groups, and consulting firms, breweries can measure themselves against Key Performance Indicators that can be applied to the brewhouse, packaging line, refrigeration system, and general operations of the building. Steps can start small, such as turning off lights in unused spaces, and can grow into installing motion sensors and high efficiency lighting. It can begin with basic maintenance, such as replacing air filters, and develop into SEER-rated, Energy Star HVAC systems. Businesses with deeper pockets can make an even greater impact by investing in brewing equipment that can recover and reuse heat energy otherwise wasted during the brewing process.

Another critical consideration, and cost sensitive one, is where the energy is coming from. Especially when considering electricity, breweries increasingly have more options for how they source their energy. Rather than purchasing electricity produced via coal or natural gas power plants, businesses can elect to purchase renewable energy, typically at a higher cost. The dramatic advances in solar energy have allowed for many breweries to explore and invest in self-supplied energy.

A destination brewery and industry leader in sustainability, Maui Brewing Company's primary production facility became fully grid-independent in 2019, drawing 100% of their energy from self-sustaining sources (Fauble, 2019). Founded in 2005 as a single brewpub in Lahaina, Hawaii, the business quickly expanded. Now, it has four locations and employs over 700 people (Clifford, 2017). With the dramatic growth, Maui Brewing co-founder Garrett Marrero took every opportunity to invest in sustainable energy. What began with leveraging tax credits for minor sustainable energy improvements grew into a four-year renewable energy project that culminated in a roof-top solar photovoltaic and solar thermal system complemented with battery packs and biodiesel fuel generators to provide the electricity and hot water necessary for brewing (Maui Brewing Company, 2019). The company has also taken strides in recycling carbon dioxide. Produced as a byproduct of the fermentation process and separately used in the packaging and carbonation of the final product, carbon dioxide plays an important role in beer. Now, 86% of the carbon dioxide used to carbonate the beer is produced, captured, and reused onsite, reducing its carbon emissions by more than two million pounds annually (Fauble, 2019).

Waste

Because of the large number of resources required to produce beer, breweries also produce considerable volumes of waste. The brewing industry has an opportunity to mitigate its impact through sustainability efforts. These waste materials include water, spent grain, spent hops, trub, yeast, caustic and acid chemical cleaners, spoiled beer, and carbon dioxide gas (Thomas & Rahman, 2006). Many of these waste products are not individually isolated but are instead discharged in combination. While this simplifies the handling of waste materials, it upsets the metric analysis as well as the consistency of treatment procedures required for waste management. For example, a routine brewhouse cleaning combines cleaning water, wasted yeast, cleaning chemicals, and unsellable beer in the discharge water.

Breweries will sometimes depend on publicly-owned water treatment facilities to handle their waste, and this can lead to negative consequences if done irresponsibly, creating process upsets and operational cost spikes. The high volumes of dissolved oxygen in brewery discharge stress the facilities, increase sludge production, and threaten discharge permit limits

(Rhode Island Department of Environmental Management, 2019). The high concentrations of total suspended solids directly impact sludge production as they are not biologically or chemically changed through these treatment facilities. Chemicals used by breweries also produce widely varied pH levels in discharge, potentially damaging sewer lines and facilities (Mercer, 2014). In addition to the damage, the brewery itself can be held liable.

Breweries depending upon municipal water treatment must regularly communicate with and understand the limitations of these facilities. Meeting discharge limits, applying for authorization, and installing monitoring points are all strategies to avoid costly problems (Effects of Breweries). Capturing wastewater for pretreatment before discharge can avoid many issues. Installing screens to capture solid wastes can allow breweries to reroute solids for reuse. Spent grains can be rerouted to agricultural partners for high quality, food-grade feed. Some breweries have used these as baking and food ingredients for their own customers (Amoriello et al., 2020). Others use the high-nutrient spent grain for soil additions and composting (Stocks et al., 2012).

Spent grain is only the beginning as any brewery producing beer creates waste simply by operating. New Belgium Brewing (NBB) takes on that challenge directly, diverting 99.9% of its waste away from landfills (Gerrard, 2018). Operations big and small were adjusted to reach this milestone. The small step of phasing out paperboard dividers in packaging resulted in a reduction of over 460 tons of paperboard used annually. Over 500 waste collection points across their brewery were audited and managed with end-of-life scenarios for the materials collected therein. Significant efforts to maximize composting and avoiding disposable products such as dishware and utensils also helped. NBB also implemented robust sustainable purchasing guidelines, ensuring that the supply chain reflects their ethics. A 2016 audit by the US Zero Waste Business Council certified the business with platinum recognition, the highest level possible (Foust, 2016).

Another form of waste that breweries contend with is their carbon footprint. Greenhouse gasses produced through the agricultural materials, water, energy, and packaging are considerable. It is estimated that alcoholic beverages, including beer, account for 0.7% of global greenhouse gas emissions when considering the complete lifecycle of the product (Shin & Searcy, 2018). The carbon dioxide produced by fermentation for just one six pack's worth of beer would take a tree two days to absorb (Thornhill, 2020). Many large breweries have ways of capturing and reusing the gas, but now even smaller producers have found ways to offset their output. Blindman Brewing, a small brewery in Alberta, Canada, took advantage of government funding through the Emissions Reduction Alberta program to invest in carbon capturing equipment produced by Earthly Labs (Khan, 2021). The technology captures the carbon dioxide produced by the yeast within the fermentation tanks, scrubs it, and compresses it to carbonate the beers during the canning process. In doing so, the brewery will likely capture about 100 metric tons of carbon dioxide, reducing their emissions and their need to purchase the gas in the future (Rieger, 2021).

Putting it all Together

As one of the earliest and most accomplished innovators in sustainable beer production, Alaskan Brewing Company (Alaskan website) has been breaking boundaries and helping craft breweries redefine what's possible since its founding in 1986. Located in Juneau, Alaska, Alaskan has a unique set of challenges given the geographic isolation and harsh climate. As explained by co-founder and brewmaster Geoff Larson, "[t]he innate beauty of where we live kind of gives us a sense of wanting to keep it that way." "We have to innovate, otherwise we're going down the wrong path. I think comfort . . . the ease of just sitting back and doing it the same way all the time, isn't what living in Alaska is about" (Wartell and Vasquez, Alaskan). Supplied by Alaska Electric Light & Power, Juneau has been powered by 99.9% renewable hydroelectric energy since 1916 by what is believed to be the very first lake tap project in the United States (Alaska Electric Light and Power Company, 2016). The city's rugged environment necessitated thinking outside the norm, something Alaskan has also embodied.

Because southeastern Alaska has very little agriculture, their spent grain did not have a local destination, which many breweries in the continental United States take for granted. Rather than put the waste into a landfill, the brewery designed and installed a grain dryer that allows them to ship the byproduct without the water weight, resulting in much lower costs. They also designed the dryer to use up to 50% of the dried grain as a supplemental fuel source, requiring less traditional fuel to operate (Scott, 2013).

In 1998, supply shortages and logistical challenges in securing carbon dioxide inspired Alaskan to become the first craft brewery in the United States to install and operate a carbon dioxide reclamation system. Capturing and cleaning the natural byproduct of yeast fermentation, Alaskan uses the gas to package beer and purge oxygen from holding tanks. They produce the gas naturally rather than burning fossil fuels while preventing over a million pounds of carbon dioxide emissions annually (Beer Powered Beer). The brewery continued to make history in 2008, becoming the first US craft brewery to install a mash filter press (Becker, 2009). This machine provides significant efficiencies, compressing the mash during the lautering process and saving over a million gallons of water and over 60,000 gallons of fuel in the first year alone. The resulting spent grain is compressed into much dryer, compact pucks.

By 2011, Alaskan began experimenting with the capabilities of their new mash press and grain fed dryers, and in 2012, they developed a first-of-its-kind spent grain biomass boiler, using the spent grain as fuel for their brewing process. In doing so, they've replaced about half of their fossil fuel use.

Alaskan has managed to create multiple, sustainable loops within their brewhouse processes, using the byproducts of their production to supply and fuel that very process. Larson believes these operations are "an indication of how the environment can influence you positively to think differently."

The craft beer industry has produced countless underdog stories of businesses working to upend the status quo, setting higher benchmarks, and resetting expectations of consumers looking for ways to better identify with and appreciate the products they consume. Craft breweries have largely embraced forward thinking and progressive policies that encompass the profit, people, and planet that they operate for. They identify closely with the local communities they operate within, communicating concern for the local environment, charities, and populations. They've helped build a cultural identity around what it means to be involved in craft beer and thus the immediate community (Grunde et al., 2014). Craft beer is embracing sustainability and helping rewrite the narrative of how a business can operate successfully while abiding by principles and ethics that extend beyond the mighty dollar.

Note

1 B Lab is a nonprofit network that certifies companies that can metrically prove their positive impact on the people, planet, and communities they operate within.

Section IV
Case Studies

9 Building Stone Brewing

Josh Newton and Greg Koch

Introduction

In a spontaneous interview with UC Television at the San Diego History Center, Greg Koch was asked to remark on the ingredients for good beer, good food, and good business. Recalling Stone Brewing's (Stone) operations, he claimed, "[W] e actually make them [beers] quite simply. We don't use fancified processes, we use very straightforward processes with really great quality but simple ingredients" (University of California Television, 2013). While making style-defining beers like Stone IPA and Arrogant Bastard Ale might have been philosophically uncomplicated for the team at Stone, the undertaking of bringing that beer to consumers at breweries and taprooms was decidedly more complex.

This chapter examines four Stone Brewing locations – Escondido (CA), San Diego's Liberty Station, Berlin (Germany), and Richmond (VA) – to elucidate the process of establishing destination breweries in diverse cities and cultures. These cases illuminate the utilization of adaptive reuse, historic preservation, and principles of sustainability by a trailblazing brewery to contribute to community and economic (re)development of neighborhoods. Stone navigated these ventures with their solution-oriented innovativeness, collaborative partnerships, and ethical standards of operation to produce public spaces rooted in local communities. In *Beer Jesus from America*, Matt Sweetwood documents the construction of Stone Brewing World Bistro & Gardens, Berlin, because he realized retrofitting the gasworks plant site would have been easier had the original developers done the same (Sweetwood, 2019). This chapter is a similar attempt to document lessons in economic and community development from the case of Stone Brewing.

Escondido: New Development and Sustainable Landscaping

In April 2005, Greg Koch claimed that Stone Brewing World Bistro & Gardens, Escondido, was "sort of like the whip cream and cherry on top" of the new Escondido Research and Technology Center. He continued, "Do we make it viable?

DOI: 10.4324/9781003371564-13

Maybe not. I think the business park is viable without us; it's just inherently cooler with us" (Gustafson, 2005). Though the brewpub is now a cornerstone of San Diego beer culture, the business park was not the original site choice. In early 2001, Stone Brewing planned to redevelop the failed Oasis Golf & Grill in nearby San Marcos. The Planning Commission and City Council supported the redevelopment, but residents feared the brewery would increase impaired drivers and noise levels. In the end, Stone abandoned the project when the Alcoholic Beverage Control advanced resident-led regulations that would make the business unfeasible (Berhman, 2001). The leadership at Stone realized a destination brewery without resident support was not in line with their philosophy.

Although the new development site in the business park had more support, at the time, it was a risk for multiple reasons. The new location was a dramatic increase from their original brewery and taproom in nearby San Marcos – from 26,500 square feet with extensions to over 50,000 square feet. The risk of the expansion was compounded by the fact that Escondido was an unknown suburb 30 miles away from Downtown San Diego, and the new site did not appear correctly on MapQuest (Koch, 2022). To complicate matters further, the site contained a detention basin.[1]

Though another team of brewers might have seen the detention basin as an inconvenience, Stone Brewing chose the business park location because of it. Working with Schmidt Design Group and Landscape+, they transformed the detention basin into the gardens and outdoor area that made the Escondido brewpub famous. The garden made use of native plants; included fruit, avocado, and olive trees for the restaurant; and introduced a riparian habitat[2] in the middle of the outdoor area. The design's incorporation of sustainability in a social space culminated with a President's Award from the American Society of Landscape Architects – San Diego (McKean, 2010) and received Sustainable Sites Initiative (SITES)[3] certification for stormwater utilization, drought tolerance, reuse of construction materials, and sustainable landscaping (Stone Brewing, 2023).

Stone Brewing continued this innovative thinking as they expanded their operations. In 2010, they opened a warehouse and distribution center, as well as a new headquarters. In March 2011, Stone worked with the former manager of La Milpa Organica to revitalize the defunct 19-acre farm as Stone Farms. The leadership at Stone Brewing even imagined developing a hotel and barrel-aging room across from the World Bistro & Gardens, but it never came to fruition due to restrictions imposed by the developer of the potential site. Though the hotel never materialized, Stone's multiple successes attracted the attention of another San Diego County developer.

Liberty Station: Redevelopment through Historic Preservation

In May 2013, Greg Koch emerged from a hidden hole in the floor to welcome guests to the new Stone Brewing World Bistro & Gardens, Liberty Station

(Koch, 2022). The hole was one of many drilled into the former Navy base mess hall floor to fill vacant space left for infrastructural pipes and wires. Though the space was meant to save time for later renovations, it was not amenable to supporting the combined weight of brewing, restaurant, and kitchen equipment – as well as Stone's signature boulders. This was one of many problems that Stone would need to overcome in the two-and-a-half-year redevelopment of the historic site.

Interestingly, Stone Brewing did not initiate redevelopment of the Liberty Station site. When the Naval Training Center closed in 1993, the City of San Diego chose the Corky McMillin Company to redevelop the site using state and federal historic tax credits. Over the next few years, the northern half of the base was renovated to maintain some semblance of its previous design. During that time, the developers approached Stone to become the redevelopment's anchor institution. After a year of convincing, Stone agreed with the caveat "[W]e've gotta be able to do it our way, we've gotta be able to do it in a way that is going to be compelling" (Koch, 2022). Though developers conceded, Stone found that state and federal historical regulations made their way difficult.

The convoluted historical redevelopment regulations can, at times, preclude reasoning. For instance, Stone encountered roadblocks in removing the ceiling of the structure. The ceiling – which had already been replaced – was nine feet above the floor, making for horrible acoustics that could ruin the restaurant atmosphere. The federal Advisory Council on Historic Preservation allowed removal of the ceiling; however, they required its replacement before opening to maintain the historic volume of the room. Realizing the economic infeasibility of those circumstances, Greg Koch, along with developers, spent the next year fighting to successfully overturn the regulation, even traveling to Washington D.C. to meet with members of Congress.

Another regulation prohibited more than four trees in the outdoor area – and required specific tree species – to maintain views of the historical façade of the building. Ironically, outdoor shade could be facilitated using any number of features – despite blockage of the façade – and thus, Stone utilized large tree boxes. Koch commented on the labyrinth of rules attached to historic preservation, "It doesn't make any sense, it is all this very limited thinking. For the next seven years you can only do it this way and then after you can do whatever you want, and we can't control it" (Koch, 2022). Redevelopment of historical spaces is heavily controlled, but that control eventually sunsets. Stone was restricted in many ways by historical regulations but eventually planted the trees they originally intended after federal control lapsed.

Despite regulatory issues, Stone created a highly functioning public space that became the economic anchor of the mixed-use Liberty Station development. A neighboring tenant claimed that only Stone Brewing could have filled that void. The brewery was "the right business . . . Their draw, their mystique – they have a cult following that is insane" (Rowe, 2013). Though a thriving reputation was important to the success of the Liberty Station location, it also took determination and innovative solutions. These lessons would become massively important in the brewery's next two ventures outside of San Diego.

Berlin: Navigating Retrofitting in the German Context

In July 2014, Greg Koch announced Stone Brewing World Bistro & Gardens, Berlin, by crushing a pile of "industrial beer" underneath a huge boulder (Stone Brewing, 2015). Stone envisaged a European site since 2009 but announced a Request for Proposals in May 2010. After inspecting 130 sites in nine countries over five years, a former gasworks plant in Mariendorf, Berlin, was chosen to house the newest World Bistro & Garden. Greg wanted to "roll up his sleeves" on a new brewery project and use Stone's renown and expertise to legitimize and further the budding craft beer scene in Europe more broadly (Sweetwood, 2019). While Stone had experience in (re)development, the German context would prove to be a unique challenge.

The retrofitting of the gasworks plant as a destination brewery began in September 2015 and initially proceeded smoothly. Of course, there were obstacles such as contaminated soil and a network of pipes below the site, but the progression to a March 2016 opening appeared to be a coming-of-age moment for Stone and American craft beer in Europe. Greg hosted an introductory event in the space during Berlin Beer Week for German craft brewers and went on a promotional tour of seven European countries. However, the celebrations ultimately gave way to frustrations as unforeseen circumstances emerged two months before opening.

The Berlin location opening faced consecutive postponements – a total of six months – due to several issues. The first of these issues – discovered during demolition of elements in the north wing – was cracks in the building wall that resulted in a temporary government-enforced shutdown for redesign and new permits. The repairs likewise delayed opening as more expensive materials were required. Next, developers were further set back when water pipes mentioned in lot plans could not be located. On top of that, contractors often arbitrarily extended completion times. These issues were frustrating and economically detrimental as Stone paid contracted employees, rent, and bank loans with no source of income.

Stone Brewing World Bistro & Gardens, Berlin, had its opening celebration in September 2016, but the damage had been done. In a 2019 blog post, Greg declared the Berlin project "Too Big, Too Bold, Too Soon" and announced the takeover of the location by BrewDog (Koch, 2019). He explained:

[T]he construction industry in Berlin is broken . . . there's a lot of bureaucracy. The U.S. has more than a bit of that, so we were prepared for it. The real challenge was the tendency of our contractors to stop everything

when a problem arose . . . Got a question? Stop everything. Unantici-
pated challenge? Stop everything. Review the contracts. Stop everything.
Reconsider. Throw the baby out with the bathwater. But most of all, stop
everything.

(Ibid.)

The German context did not align with the aspirations of the American brewery. Thomas Tyrell, head brewer of the Berlin location, explained the mis-
alignment as such: "It's a different style of working. It's [the American style]
a very optimistic way of approaching things. And the German style is a little
bit different, seeing the problems first and try to solve them" (Sweetwood,
2019). In the end, the divergent understandings of redevelopment – timeta-
bles, processes, and solutions – between Stone and Berlin were too much to
overcome.

However, Stone's Berlin project was not a failure. Stone beers are still
brewed and distributed from the site, and sales have grown every year –
excluding the pandemic. Stone also takes solace in wins such as hosting the
most extensive craft beer selection in Germany at the time, the continuation
of that site by BrewDog, and their contribution to accelerating the craft beer
market in Germany (Koch, 2019). Likewise, Stone was pushing forward with
another project outside of San Diego.

Richmond: Redeveloping to Revitalize a Historic Neighborhood

In a 2014 video, Stone described their Escondido location as "the last brewery we'll ever need" and announced their destination brewery in Richmond,
Virginia, as "the *next* last brewery we'll ever need" (Stone Brewing, 2014).
The search for the Richmond site progressed faster than other Stone locations.
It took nine months to send a Request for Proposals, visit over 40 locations,
narrow the choice to Columbus (OH), Norfolk (VA), and Richmond (VA),
and chose the final site. Richmond topped the list because its "vibrant energy
and impressive craft beer culture, along with the uniqueness of the property"
(Stone Brewing, 2023) allowed revitalization "while honoring its historical
significance" (Hernandez). Others believed Stone could positively intervene
as well.

Politicians, community members, and the beer community in Richmond
supported Stone. Locals were ecstatic about revitalization of the area. Virginia
Governor, Terry McAuliffe, "wooed" Stone to Richmond as he appreci-
ated the economic growth breweries spurred in Asheville, North Carolina
(Hernandez, 2014). The mayor of Richmond and City Council president
were highly supportive as well, claiming "It's nice for our cool factor, but it's
great for our bottom line" (Hernandez). Dru Gillie of Richmond's Fulton Hill

Community Association added his approval of Stone Brewing's approach to "civic responsibility while having a great time doing it" (Ibid.). Stone seemingly had unanimous community support.

Still, Stone wanted to respect Fulton's history in redevelopment of the area. Greater Fulton, the site of the Richmond location, was a traditionally African-American community up to 1970. Early in the 1970s, flooding damaged much of the community, and it was targeted for urban renewal. As with similar plans motivated by racism, a thriving neighborhood with restaurants, retail shops, and homes was demolished for new construction. Fulton met the same fate of urban renewal projects in marginalized communities around the country: renewal never came.

Though neglected for decades, the majority African-American community hoped Stone could be an anchor of redevelopment. City Council member, Cynthia Newbile, claimed Fulton had been "living on a dream deferred . . . that gave people hope that someday they might return to a renewed and rebuilt neighborhood . . . it feels like those dreams and promises may finally be coming true after 40 years of waiting and hoping" (Hernandez). A resident, Juliellen Sarver, believed Stone could facilitate "respect after so many years of disrespect" (Ibid.). Stone humbly attempted to fulfill community desires while respecting its history. For instance, during excavation, Stone found a water boiler and chunks of concrete and used them as decoration at the brewery to respect the community that occupied the space before.

Stone desired to economically revitalize the area as well. Stone leadership hoped to directly affect community prospects by creating 288 jobs in the brewery and restaurant. In mid-2016, Stone opened the brewery, taproom, and store, and in 2018, Stone discussed renovating buildings to house their restaurant and gardens. This second phase of the project was tabled due to affordability (Robinson, 2019), but in March 2022, Stone increased its production with four new tanks (Becker, March 2022). In June 2022, during the writing of this chapter, Stone Brewing was bought by Sapporo USA. While many in Richmond feared what this might mean for economic development, Sapporo claimed it intended to honor previous leases, double facility production, and invest $20–$40 million into the location (Becker, July 2022). It remains unclear what will become of the plan to construct a restaurant and gardens.

Building Destination Breweries, the Stone Brewing Way

In Stone Brewing's 26 years of creating breweries and taprooms in California, Virginia, Germany, and China, they have learned to navigate different contexts and cultures of (re)development. The aforementioned cases show Stone's ability to innovate solutions to problems, harness collaborative partnerships, operate ethically, and develop and maintain a local connectedness. This section elaborates upon these themes.

Solution-Oriented Innovativeness

In (re)development of locations, Stone displayed a penchant for innovating solutions to procedural issues. Solutions-oriented approaches are common in sustainability science as scholars understand that "generating solutions to sustainability challenges lies in a plural way of thinking" (Tengö & Anderson, 2002, p. 28). These approaches rely on multiple spheres of knowledge to address problems. Greg Koch said it best when discussing the Berlin location:

> Any time you attempt to build something with the size and scope of Stone Berlin, you're going to run into unexpected challenges . . . But we've been able to grow Stone Brewing because we figure it out as quickly as possible. We always keep moving, keep working. We never stop. Never. And trust me, we're no problem-solving geniuses. We consult smarter people, accept acceptable solutions, just get it done.
>
> (Koch, 2019)

For example, Stone viewed the detention basin at the Escondido site as an opportunity instead of a problem; however, it was an opportunity they needed help to fully realize. As such, Stone relied on the knowledge of a landscape architecture and planning group to develop an innovative solution.

A solutions-orientation also requires delving into actions atypical of one's normal operations. Stone participated in a historic preservation project at Liberty Station with problematic regulations that curtailed the vision of the brewery. As mentioned, Greg Koch explored policy advocacy at the state and federal level to overturn historic room volume regulations. Instead of succumbing to rigid regulations, he pursued a collaborative solution with the agencies in control.

Collaborative Partnerships

Stone Brewing knew when to seek collaborative partnerships and harness community support for projects. Influential urban planner, Patsy Healey, claimed that collaborative relationships in place-making should integrate diverse agendas, be inclusive of multiple stakeholders, use multiple forms of knowledge, and build "relational resources" (Healey, 1998, p. 1536). The aforementioned cases exhibit Stone's ability to utilize each of these collaborative practices in establishing public places. Stone integrated diverse agendas throughout its projects including economic redevelopment of neighborhoods through adaptive reuse, engagement with historic memory and preservation, and environmentally sustainable landscaping. Stone was likewise inclusive of multiple stakeholders in their projects including developers, public officials, architects and planners, and residents.

Stone Brewing's utilization of multiple knowledges and relational resources was illustrated in the example of the detention basin, but the Berlin location presents another example. During the retrofitting of the gasworks plant, multiple issues arose from unforeseen circumstances. While Greg understood the business aspect of (re)development, he knew construction was not his forte. He therefore relied on his relational resources and flew the Stone Brewing Director of Construction and Facilities to Berlin to motivate contractors to progress the project more efficiently (Sweetwood, 2019). Harnessing collaborative partnerships resulted in better place-making in all Stone locations and produced quicker solutions.

Ethical Operation

Stone Brewing is guided by a philosophy that industrialization and commodification of beer and food creates inferior products. This was a deeply personal realization for Greg Koch who struggled with debilitating gastrointestinal issues through his teens and 20s resulting from consumption of processed foods (Stone Brewing, 2016). In fact, Greg communicated his frustration with food systems in his UC Television interview:

> The concept that in today's world . . . that a simple level of standards when it comes to simple quality, purity, actual real food being that minimum standard . . . just like the idea that the simple barley, water, hops, and yeast and nothing else that is in this beer . . . that this could qualify as snobbery . . . is a ridiculous notion.

(UCTV)

This frustration produced an ethic that guided Stone's operations and development of locations.

Stone's approach to beer was most representative of this ethos. They committed to brewing quality beer with simple ingredients no matter the cost. After their first year of brewing, they were losing over $30,000 monthly because their bold flavors were unconventional (Stone Brewing, 2012). Likewise, part of the reason the Berlin location did not work is that the German market was somewhat resistant to a higher price for quality beer (Koch, 2019). Stone Brewing's persistence in these moments is indicative of their understanding that beer should be ethically produced despite market consequences.

These ethics can also be seen in the revitalization of the defunct local organic farm, La Milpa Organica. Farm manager David Solomon used biodynamic management techniques to ensure the produce was locally sourced and the final product was completely organic (McKean, 2011). Stone's commitment to organic food went beyond their own restaurants' needs though. In

September 2011, they began selling excess produce to community residents, and in June 2013, Stone opened the farm to the public on weekends as a form of environmental education. Stone's commitment to what Koch called "real" food pushed them beyond brewing into community-based farming.

Just as Stone believed food and beer should not do harm to people's guts or palates, their style of (re)development tried to accomplish the same. The company experienced the difficulty of development against community wishes in the search for their Escondido site. This influenced them to seek willing participants in future site searches. Even when there was overwhelming community support, such as in Richmond, Stone learned to delicately deal with historic trauma in their (re)development.

Local Rootedness

This concern for the communities where they locate is guided by a desire to be locally rooted. Since the 1992 UN Conference on Environment and Development, there has been a push to assert differing degrees of local control over development processes; although, scholars claim that we should not fall into the "local trap" of assuming all local processes are socially just and environmentally sustainable (Purcell & Brown, 2005, pp. 279–280). While Stone's development processes do not implement the highest degree of community participation, their actions are based in a desire to garner local support. This is best reflected in their Request for Proposals process, which seeks community voices.

Stone also uses locally sourced materials to root their establishments in the locality and contribute to the sustainability of their development and business processes. Their use of local-sourced organic produce, as well as use of local species of plants in their gardens, was mentioned previously; however, Stone Brewing also utilizes local materials and art – even local fan art – as the decorative elements of their destination breweries. Likewise, the signature boulders – or stones – at every location are typically taken from the development site, along with other objects found during excavation, to symbolize the foundation that Stone attempts to establish in the community.

Most important in this regard is Stone Brewing's actual engagement with local communities. For example, in San Diego, their giving to local nonprofit and community-based organizations such as Fight ALD, the Boys & Girls Club of San Marcos, Surfrider Foundation, CSUSM Foundation, Big Brothers Big Sisters of San Diego County, North County Food Bank, and others often exceeded $500,000 annually. This giving goes beyond the $3 million in donations of beer to local events. Additionally, Stone was well-known for promoting local breweries through their distribution company, their collaborative brewing efforts, and the local guest taps at every restaurant. Finally, Stone created community locally through events such as dinners pairing local produce with beer or their annual anniversary festivals that took over the California State University-San Marcos campus. From their site selection to the construction of locations to their engagement in charity and events, Stone exemplified place-making rooted in local communities.

Final Thoughts: "Be Different to Be Better"

As mentioned, Stone Brewing was sold to Sapporo USA during the writing of this chapter, making it a perfect time to take stock of what Stone accomplished and learn from its experiences. This chapter highlighted four cases of Stone Brewing's (re)development of sites – Escondido, Liberty Station, Berlin, and Richmond – for destination breweries through urban planning techniques such as adaptive reuse, historic preservation, and community and economic development. The brewery largely accomplished this through principles of solutions-oriented innovation, collaboration with multiple types of stakeholders, ethical operation, and rootedness in local communities. Some final thoughts help make these lessons more practical for stakeholders involved in the (re)development of locations as destination breweries.

Greg Koch once summed up Stone Brewing's success:

Don't be different to be different . . . be different to be better" (Stone Brewing Co. Greg Koch Talks at Google). For economic and community developers and other public officials, this means being solutions-oriented as Stone Brewing was. It should not solely be breweries leading in this capacity. In an interview for this chapter, Koch lamented the fact that "there are so many [public officials] that think their job is to say no."

(Koch, 2022)

These cases highlight that though regulations are necessary, some are outdated and hold back the economic, social, and environmental development of neighborhoods. Instead of rigid adherence regardless of context, public officials can utilize a solutions orientation to critically think through the necessity of specific regulations. See chapters 10 and 11 for more on how cities have dealt with regulations in relation to brewery development.

For breweries, context is incredibly important. One aspect of this is scale: "[D]o you want to build your brewery to be a Stone or are you happy enough with one small location . . . that is still an asset to the community?" (Koch, 2022). The other side is knowing the context in which you are developing. Some neighborhoods will always be off-limits to breweries because of price. Others will be hard to establish a presence in because of the reputation of craft beer. For instance, Koch believes that Los Angeles has been slow to develop a beer scene because of the failure of early brewery projects. And yet context is not everything. San Diego was not ready for Stone Pale Ale, and the community continued to question Stone Brewing's aggressiveness in flavor as Stone IPA and Arrogant Bastard Ale entered the scene. The same was true at the Berlin location. Nonetheless, reminiscing on lessons learned, Koch claimed, "I believe in not listening to the public if you want to do something great, you've gotta listen to yourself and then people that support your vision will follow you" (Stone Brewing, 2012). Though it took decades to manifest, Stone Brewing successfully created locally rooted destination breweries that provide important lessons for those that follow in their footsteps.

Notes

1 Detention basins help manage stormwater and protect against flooding in 100-year flood zones.
2 Riparian habitats are zones between land and water sources that utilize vegetation to reduce soil erosion from floods and increase biodiversity in an area.
3 For more information, see https://sustainablesites.org.

10 Municipal Regulatory Reform for Beer Industry Growth

A City's Experience

Russ Gibbon

San Diego County has been referred to as "America's Beer Capital," "The Craft Beer Capital of America," "the Nation's Craft Beer Capital," "the Capital of Craft," and similar terms and deservedly so (Elder, 2010; Rowe, 2010; San Diego Brewers Guild, 2023). According to the California State University at San Marcos, as of 2021, San Diego County had 158 licensed beer companies in operation, more than any other county in the United States (Concepcion, 2019). Approximately half of these are in the city of San Diego, which has a long history of supporting the industry. The beer industry in San Diego traces back to 1868 when Christian and Martha Dobler established the first local brewery, Pioneer Chollas Valley Brewery, on farmland thought to be near the current interchange of the 15 and 94 Freeways (Kaplan, 2018, p. 2). Early in the 20th Century, several other notable beer companies built breweries and brewpubs in the city, including San Diego Brewing Company and Aztec Brewing Company, both in the Barrio Logan neighborhood, and Mission Brewery in the Middletown neighborhood (Kaplan, 2018, pp. 3–5). These breweries were welcomed into San Diego without any special permitting process other than standard ministerial building and grading permits (City of San Diego Municipal Code).

Prohibition and later the market dominance of major beer companies and consumer tastes led to the ultimate demise of the local breweries until 1978 when changes to state and federal laws led to the proliferation of homebrewers in San Diego. The year 1989 is regarded as the beginning of the "modern era" for the beer industry in San Diego as that is when Matt Rattner and Chris Cramer established Karl Strauss Brewing Company in downtown San Diego. Several other beer companies including AleSmith Brewing Company, San Diego Brewing Company, Home Brew Mart, Inc., and Oggi's Pizza and Brewing Company opened up brewpubs and microbreweries in suburban San Diego locations north of the 8 Freeway during the early to mid-1990's. AleSmith, notably, was the first to establish itself in the Miramar industrial park area, which now has the county's largest production breweries and the largest concentration of breweries, colloquially referred to as "Beeramar" (Contreras, 2019, pp. 1–2).

DOI: 10.4324/9781003371564-14

The city of San Diego first began its active support of the local beer industry by assisting Ballast Point with its expansion into the Scripps Ranch Business Park in the Scripps Miramar Ranch community in 2004. This expansion into a 20,000-square-foot former tool and die factory constituted a major leap forward for the industry, becoming the second-largest brewery in the city during the "modern era," following eight years after Karl Strauss had constructed its 20,000-square-foot production brewery in the city's Pacific Beach neighborhood. City staff from the Community & Economic Development and Development Services departments collaborated to resolve building code and parking issues, which enabled Ballast Point to add a 50-barrel brewing system, outdoor tanks, a relatively large indoor tasting room (large at that time!), and the first outdoor tasting area ("patio"). The city's municipal code regulations imposed some restrictions on "Eating and Drinking Establishments" within industrial zones, but the city staff determined that the outdoor beer drinking use was accessory to the primary beer manufacturing use (thus no change in use); therefore, the previously conforming parking spaces were deemed adequate. No special permit or variance was required.

By 2011, the city staff became aware that two businesses were looking for industrial space to expand capacity. Ballast Point Brewing & Spirits was rapidly outgrowing its Scripps Ranch brewery, and production was maxing out at its original Home Brew Mart location in the Linda Vista community. Additionally, yeast manufacturer White Labs, which was operating from a small suite in a Miramar multi-tenant industrial building, was looking to triple its manufacturing capacity. White Labs, one of the nation's largest yeast producers, manufactures yeast for fermented beverages like beer, wine, and cider, with beer yeast being their primary product. This was truly the beginning of the "craft beer" renaissance.

At that time, the city's economic development employees were part of the mayor's office, due to a reorganization in 2009. The reorganization was initiated by Mayor Jerry Sanders who, after having stabilized the city's moribund financial situation, wanted to make economic growth a focus of his second term. The new Economic Growth Services unit thus had direct access to not only the mayor but also the mayor's senior operations managers, department directors, and his policy advisors and media relations staff. Fortuitously, Mayor Sanders was also known by his staff to be a craft beer aficionado.

Having been informed that White Labs' unprecedented expansion presaged a subsequent tripling of yeast production, with San Diego uniquely positioned to grab more than its fair share of industry growth, the mayor gave the green light to his policy, media, and economic development staff to "push the envelope" to make sure that San Diego would be the "capital city of the beer industry." In June 2011, staff gathered local industry leaders such as Colby Chandler of Ballast Point Brewing, Mike and Lisa Hinkley of Green Flash Brewing, Lisa White of White Labs, and Adam Carbonell, president of the

San Diego Brewers Guild. Standing in Green Flash's new 45,000-square-foot brewery (largest in San Diego at the time), the mayor famously proclaimed "June is Craft Beer Month in San Diego" and that "if you're 21 or over, and you drink beer, it's your civic duty to support local brewers." The event was covered by on-air, online, and print media.

Over the course of the next three years, city staff actively chased the beer industry, facilitating the attraction and expansion not only of White Labs but also of major production breweries such as Coronado Brewing Company, Hess Brewing Company, Modern Times Beer Company, Societe Brewing Company, and Saint Archer Brewing Company, all of which opened 20–30-barrel brewhouses. These were in addition to existing 30–50-barrel brewhouses operated by Ballast Point, Karl Strauss, and Mission Brewery. In each case, staff assisted the company expansions by exploiting "previously conforming" code regulations so that brewers would not incur expensive parking requirements or traffic impact fees.

By 2013, it was becoming obvious that the regulatory "low hanging fruit" had already been plucked, and the city's Municipal Code provisions ("zoning code") would hinder industry growth. It had also become evident to city staff that the city's fastest growing and most commercially successful brewery, Ballast Point Brewing & Spirits, was going to run headlong into code-based roadblocks for which there was no easy work-around or "loopholes" such as creative interpretations of the code.

Ballast Point identified an old art gallery in Little Italy, which the company figured (correctly) would make an ideal location for its third brewery. Little Italy is well known as a tourist destination due to its many high-end restaurants and bars, historical ambiance and location near downtown, the waterfront, airport, and trolley line. However, it was located within the highly regulated "Centre City Planned District," which has a unique zoning code within the city's municipal code. Due to long-standing concerns regarding public inebriation in this highly urbanized area, special discretionary Conditional Use Permits (CUP) were required for any establishment that would sell alcoholic beverages for onsite consumption or "to go," with the exception of full-scale restaurants ("bona fide eating place"). Mission Brewery had gone through the CUP process in 2012 and, not surprisingly, found it to be long, drawn out, and costly. Upon receiving it, the permit contained all manner of restrictions on operations. The economic development staff met with Ballast Point's founders Jack White, Yuseff Cherney, and new CEO Jim Buechler to discuss how the city could best support the new venture. Staff suggested that Ballast Point circumvent the CUP process by adding a kitchen such that the establishment would meet the criteria for a "bona fide eating place." Ballast Point's executives agreed that they would rather invest in a food service component than in a comparably expensive and time-consuming CUP process. This solved one problem, but "to-go" sales of bottled beer and growlers was a necessary component of the cash flows needed to make the project feasible in this high-rent district. The code provided no exceptions. The economic development staff promised to pursue a code change to allow "brewpubs" to sell beer for off-site consumption. Trusting city staff to follow through on this commitment, Ballast Point leased the building, remodeled it into a brewpub, and opened in 2013.

The economic development staff took the opportunity to pursue other changes to the Center City Planned District Ordinance. Breweries would still require a discretionary permit, but the process level was reduced to a Neighborhood Development Permit ("NDP"), which, while discretionary and subject to compliance with the California Environmental Quality Act ("CEQA"), does not require a public hearing and is several thousand dollars cheaper to process. These code changes were completed in 2014 (O-20368 SDMC, 2014, p. 49).

At the same time that Ballast Point was seeking to open the Little Italy brewpub, the company was also planning for a large, new production facility. Sales of its flagship product, Sculpin IPA, had taken off, and the Scripps Ranch brewery could not meet the demand for a product that was now being shipped nationwide. Ballast Point was in negotiations with a developer to build a large purpose-built brewery/restaurant similar to Stone Brewing Company's "Brewery Gardens." The new brewery was proposed in the neighboring city of Poway and would include a 15,000-square-foot restaurant and tasting room. Ballast Point informed the city of San Diego staff that it was also considering a lease of the old Van Can Company building in the Miramar area, but that the building was "rather rough" and generally unattractive for use as a brewery that would include a large restaurant component. It was, however, a central location for retail purposes and a much cheaper option as compared to the developer's build-to-suit proposal in the city of Poway, and it could be remodeled quickly, accelerating time to market for Sculpin IPA and other in-demand company products. City staff was also aware that the proposed mezzanine addition would require more off-street parking on a constrained site, that the code also limited "eating and drinking establishments" to no more than 3,000 feet, and that traffic fees would be a significant cost issue as well.

City staff in the Development Services department (which now included the Economic Development division) proposed the 2013 "Microbrewery Ordinance," which included a new exception to the 3,000-square-foot limitation for "Eating and Drinking Establishments." The new footnote to the Use Regulations Table provided the following exception:

Industrial development greater than 12,000 square feet of gross floor area that is primarily engaged in the manufacturing of malt beverages or distilled spirits in sealed cans, bottles, or kegs, may include an eating and drinking establishment as an accessory use, subject to applicable state and local regulations, if the eating and drinking establishment does not exceed 25 percent of the gross floor area of the structures on the premises.

(O-20262 SDMC, 2013, pp. 1–3)

This city council-approved code change was also designed to accommodate the retention and expansion of AleSmith Brewing Company, which was considering a lease of the old vacant Hoist Fitness Company manufacturing plant, also in the Miramar area. AleSmith intended to construct either a large on-site restaurant or a very large tasting room within a huge brewery. To further augment the proposed regulatory relief, the city staff also offered both companies other inducements or "incentives" to locate their major production breweries in Miramar, including inclusion in an expanded California Enterprise Zone, expedited permitting, and reimbursement of traffic impact fee costs using sales, use, and property tax revenue derived from the new projects. Both companies ultimately signed long-term leases for the vacant 100,000+-square-foot manufacturing plants and invested tens of millions of dollars in property, plant, and equipment. Ballast Point expanded its facility from 106,000 square feet to 126,000 square feet, which included a 14,000-square-foot full-scale restaurant, and AleSmith ultimately built out its new 105,000-square-foot facility to include a massive two-level 25,000-square-foot tasting room. The city's support of both companies provided the desired result as Miramar was then anchored by what had become California's 6th and 8th largest breweries. Ten more breweries opened nearby these two during the next few years.

In 2015, the economic development staff included language relating to parking in a comprehensive code update ordinance, which would be beneficial to both the beer and biotech industries. The modified parking ratio went from 2.5 off-street parking spaces per 1,000 square feet of gross floor area ("GFA") to only 1 space/1,000 square feet of GFA (O-20481 SDMC, 2015, pp. 70–71). Since an off-street parking space, whether surface or structured, costs a minimum of $10,000 each, this change alone made infeasible projects feasible. Because the change was limited to manufacturing uses only, rather than an across-the-board reduction for all land uses, the benefit inured to manufacturers as lessees (tenants), not to industrial property owners (landlords). What is important to understand is that the city made these changes and provided perhaps hundreds of hours of direct support and problem resolution at a time when local breweries needed these accommodations and cost savings at critical junctures in their growth.

Additional changes in 2015 permitted live entertainment and the installation of tanks and equipment (such as grain towers, fermentation tanks, hot and cold "liquor" tanks and other appurtenances) without the normally required screening from the public right-of-way. While perhaps seemingly minor, this latter change was important not only because the screening of 30–50-foot tall tanks and towers would be costly but also because these tanks were often painted with the company logo as part of the "look" of a brewery (O-20481 SDMC, 2015, pp. 53, 70, 71).

As the most salient example of city-supported growth, Ballast Point went from about 40 employees in early 2013 to almost 400 employees in 2015. That year, the company was sold to Constellation Brands for a staggering $1 billion. Following that sale, Ballast Point's CEO Jim Buechler gave credit to the city of San Diego during a 2016 interview at his alma mater, Harvard Business School: "Our pro-craft beer San Diego City government has created and nurtured an environment where 115-plus local breweries work together to create some of the best craft beer in the country" (Rhenish et al., 1).

Hess (now "Mike Hess") Brewing Company's original location was also in the Miramar area. Mike Hess had identified a vacant bookstore in the North Park community for his second and much larger new brewery. However, in 2012, manufacturing was generally not a permitted use in commercial zones. Although restaurants of any size were considered permitted uses, Hess had no desire to operate a brewpub. Bakeries were a permitted use within this Mid-City Planned District, so economic development staff successfully convinced the Development Services department director to approve the use, based on the logic that beer was "liquid bread" since both products are primarily made using grain, water, and yeast. This creative interpretation later permitted Fall Brewing Company, Poorhouse Brewing Company, and North Park Brewing Company to establish breweries in this community. However, by 2015, North Park was undergoing a Community Plan Update, which would involve replacing the Planned District Ordinance with "citywide zoning," in particular with a series of commercial zones that did not permit manufacturing of any kind.

In an effort to continue to permit breweries and other craft beverage and food producers in commercial areas such as North Park where redevelopment was occurring and they were desired as an amenity, a new land use was created in order to ensure land use compatibility. The staff proposed, and the city council approved, a new Separately Regulated Industrial Use entitled: "Artisan Food & Beverage Producer." An entire new section was added to the code, which permitted the use, in most instances ministerially (aka "by right"), but with limitations and restrictions designed to avoid the land use conflicts that so frequently occur when manufacturing operations are directly adjacent to residential units (O-20752 SDMC, 10-11).

Also, in 2015, beer manufacturers were increasingly interested in selling beer at retail locations in neighborhoods, particularly when their brewery and its accessory tasting room was located in relatively remote auto-oriented industrial parks. The California Business and Professions Code regulates all production, distribution, and sales of alcoholic beverages in the state. These regulations are administered by the California Department of Alcoholic Beverage Control (ABC), which issues all licenses for these business activities pursuant to that state code. Type 01 Beer Manufacturers and Type 23 Small

Beer Manufacturers are allowed to "duplicate" their licenses to sell beer in company stores referred to in the Business & Professions Code as "satellite offices." Although the state business code was later amended, at that time, ABC was required to issue "duplicate licenses" to beer manufacturers "forthwith," with no opportunity for law enforcement or community stakeholders to protest the license prior to issuance. The city staff wanted to allow the establishment of the beer stores, but to balance a business-friendly approach with some level of regulations to prevent a politically-driven regulatory backlash from land use conflicts that might otherwise occur, a new land use was again proposed by staff and approved by the city council:

> Retail tasting stores are branch locations of an affiliated licensed beer manufacturer, which sell or deliver alcoholic beverages produced by that manufacturer. Consumption of the applicable beverage may be on or off the premises of the retail tasting store. Retail tasting stores are establishments with Duplicate Type 1 Beer Manufacturer Licenses or a Duplicate Type 23 Small Beer Manufacturer Licenses issued by the California Department of Alcoholic Beverage Control. This Section does not apply to tasting rooms located on the premises of a licensed beer manufacturer. No beer manufacturing shall occur on the premises of the retail tasting store.
> (O-20481 SDMC, 2015, p. 57)

Since about 2011, the city of San Diego's economic development employees had been collecting relevant metrics to show the strength of the local industry, mainly to justify various forms of regulatory relief or for the creation of programs and initiatives to support the industry. By 2019, it was time to declare victory and begin marketing the city of San Diego as the Beer Capital of the World. An interactive map was created for the city's website, making it possible to click on a location and, in most instances, see the number of employees, square footage occupied, the size of the brewing system, and the number of barrels of beer produced annually. In the aggregate, by 2018, the city had 83 breweries operating a total of 108 separate establishments, including 57 breweries, 29 brewpubs (beer production + prepared food), and 21 retail tasting stores (aka "beer stores," "tasting rooms," "taprooms," etc.). Six of these beer companies were licensed by the California Department of Alcoholic Beverages as Type 01 Beer Manufacturers (60,000+ barrels annually). Within the city, these 83 breweries occupied just over 1 million square feet of commercial or industrial space, produced over 800,000 barrels of beer annually, and employed 849 employees.

In general, the city of San Diego has embraced and supported its local beer industry for over 150 years. Beer production, from the home brewer through major production breweries, has been a part of San Diego's culture. What started in the city of San Diego later spread to almost every other jurisdiction in San Diego County by the time of this writing. From 2011 onward, the city of San Diego, including its staff and its highest-ranking elected officials, took bold and visible actions to ensure that local brewers could start up and expand operations with the fewest possible bureaucratic hurdles and government costs. Regulatory relief measures proposed by the mayor and his staff were always approved by the city council unanimously. The city's planners, engineers, and managers in multiple departments made extra efforts and took risks to creatively interpret codes and implement programs and policies specifically designed to support the beer industry. These efforts paid significant dividends to the city in terms of increased tax revenue, the creation of middle-income blue collar job opportunities for residents, and increased tourism and, in many instances, contributed to urban revitalization. San Diego's beer industry is as well recognized throughout the world as Napa and Sonoma Counties are recognized for their wine industry.

11 Craft Breweries and the City of Vista

Cultivating Industry Growth From Within Municipal Government

Kevin Ham

What does it take to successfully foster craft brewing industry growth from within the halls of municipal government? The city of Vista, a Southern California suburban community with a population of about 99,000 residents, has one of the highest breweries per capita ratios in the country. This was no accident – reaching this unique status has been a multistage process of cultivating industry support and partnership from city officials. Led by the Vista director of economic development, with the support of the director of community development and others in the city, Vista officials took the time to listen to what brewery owners and entrepreneurs wanted to do and what was needed and then worked with them to accomplish it. After determining how to support the craft beer industry and recognize the value of breweries to the city, the approach was to have the breweries work with a single city staff person to better accomplish growth and overcome challenges. Stabilizing the industry once they had enough breweries to have a critical mass was also key – this included working with the breweries on identifying and revising municipal codes and county and state regulations that could hinder growth (see also Chapter 10). Lastly, the final stage focuses on how city officials will continue to help the industry grow and what support is necessary.

Before we discuss what the City of Vista did to identify, support, and grow the craft brewing industry, it is best to give a brief overview of what an Economic Development Department does. At the city level, economic development is the process of improving the economic well-being of a community. How a jurisdiction does this differs based on its local industries, employment pool, and governmental goals and objectives. Economic development programs can focus on job creation and training, business recruitment, business retention, and facilitating an understanding of government processes and solving challenges that businesses may face (Ombudsman activities), to name a few. This is the main framework for which a city supports growing its economy and enhancing the prosperity and quality of life for all in the community. The strategies and tools employed to meet these goals can vary widely

DOI: 10.4324/9781003371564-15

from city to city and across states. In a few rare circumstances, cities get the opportunity to help grow an emerging industry. This requires greater flexibility and risk that are associated more often with the private sector but can be accomplished by a municipality as has been done in Vista with the amazing craft brewing and craft makers communities. In this chapter, we are happy to share our path that we took as well as moving forward.

Discovering the Craft Beer Industry

The question the City of Vista receives most often is "Why Vista?" The answer is simple, because, as a city, we took the time to listen to what a growing industry wanted to do and what they needed and worked with them to accomplish it. Taking the time to understand if a community can support a specific use and if and how to assist them is a very important function of an Economic Development Department. This is what helps cities with finding the next industry that may grow or expand and to employ residents.

As a city, Vista discovered the industry in the early 2000s when a Vista Council member invited the new Economic Development director to Stone Brewing's annual party at their headquarters in the neighboring city of San Marcos, California. When we saw the activity and enthusiasm they had generated in a commercial warehouse, we understood that this really could be a way to support the Vista Business Park and spur growth in our downtown. Also, around this same time, the City of Vista had started a new Economic Development Strategy, which envisioned expansion of our Vista Business Park and ways to enliven our historic downtown. We thought the craft brewing industry could create a new manufacturing sector while at the same time supporting existing employers and employees in the park. We believed that the businesses in the park would find it easier to retain and attract talented employees if they had breweries nearby to support local companies' creative energies and social interactions. In the downtown district, we believed the industry could draw more visitors and shoppers, and it had the potential to help us revitalize some of the areas we were working on to create an active city center. The city's new Economic Development Strategy also called for supporting the biotech industry, and the Economic Development staff was able to make a connection between this goal and the craft brewing industry for city leadership such that the craft brewing industry fell into this category and should be supported. Those city leaders that needed to be convinced that this industry should be supported, and our efforts began in earnest. Sometimes, it takes creativity and risk to move forward on new fronts even at the city-government level, and as can be seen by the craft brewing industry's growth, it worked here. The first two breweries in Vista (both started in 2002) could not have been more different. One was a restaurant with a brewery (Lamppost Pizza/Back Street Brewery), and the other was a beer manufacturer with a tasting room (Green Flash Brewery). These two breweries gave us a chance to see how the different brewery uses could support our thesis of the value of the breweries in different environments benefitting our community.

The Early Days: Determining How to Support the Craft Beer Industry and Their Value

What we think of as "Breweries 2.0" in Vista include our third and fourth breweries, which were Mother Earth and Iron Fist, both starting in 2010. They were both located in a more industrial/commercial area, and we thought they would support the Vista Business Park businesses and employees, and this turned out to be true, and more.

Once these two breweries were established, the proverbial floodgates were opened. We started to gain new breweries quickly. In addition to an active and energizing environment created by these establishments, the two new breweries and the other two original breweries became our industry champions and evangelized why Vista was the place to locate your brewery. Home brewers who wanted to open a brewery would ask the owners how they were able to open since they were turned down in other municipalities. When this question was asked, they would be sent directly to the city's Economic Development team for assistance. It should also be noted that Mother Earth had a home brew store at this time, and many want-to-be brewery owners would gather there to share ideas on beers and locations, and the default location of choice was Vista, due to the city's understanding and support of the craft brewing industry. Vista is also proud that many breweries in the northern part of San Diego County and the City of San Diego made their first stop in Vista to talk to the city staff about operations for when they locate in another city.

Vista could not accommodate all the growth of these requests to locate in the city, so the Vista Economic Development team worked with other jurisdictions to forward many of these future tasting rooms and breweries to their communities. The City of Vista assisted these municipalities in understanding the unique needs of the industry and how to work within city codes to accommodate their placement within different zones. The City of Vista staff worked with these breweries from all over San Diego, creating goodwill, lifetime connections, and friends within the brewing community. The team of staff that was involved in these efforts is proud of the changes that emerged from their continued connections to, and support of, the craft brewing community. It is the author's personal view that a new and more flexible way of addressing all businesses grew from our mutual efforts to understand and grow this industry.

Once Vista had five or six breweries, perceived and real issues started to arise, due to the industry's quick growth. These potential impacts included additional law enforcement support due to drunk driving and a perception that bar-related issues would proliferate, city budget issues related to added costs of additional staffing needed to monitor and oversee the industry, discussions on how many breweries were too many (saturation point), conflicts with surrounding business traffic patterns, additional law enforcement needs during the weekends (when business parks are typically vacant), food trucks and their need to stay at breweries for an extended time, and more. Some of these were perceived issues such as where alcohol is served, law enforcement will need to be there frequently or real issues such as ordinance changes to allow for food trucks to stay in a location for an extended period. To tackle these issues, the owner of Mother Earth (Dan Love) and the city's Economic Development director formed the Vista Brewers Guild (VBG) so the industry could speak with one voice and work with the city on relevant issues. This partnership also allowed the city to work with all breweries at the same time on most issues to establish industry standards agreed to by most participants. Yet sometimes, there were outlier issues that needed to be addressed separately, and we did.

Tackling the Issues

How the city tackled perceived and real issues is important to explore, so this next section will take a brief look at each by examining two specific issues.

1. Perceived issue: anytime alcohol is served, law enforcement will need to be there frequently

While it is true that alcohol service can increase the need for law enforcement, careful management, oversight, and proper policies can greatly reduce the frequent need for their services. It should also be noted that different alcohol license types can bring different customers and their corresponding issues. At the start of the craft brewing expansion in Vista and in San Diego County, there was no track record for what type of customer behaviors would be seen, so a slow and thoughtful approach was taken. For the most part, jurisdictions saw positive customer behaviors that were very different than that of bars and have implemented codes and policies for tasting rooms and breweries that are less stringent than other types of alcohol service establishments.

But as indicated, at the onset, this was unknown, so Vista implemented several requirements at the start of the industry growth. These included much more limited hours than are allowed today, drunk-driving tracking and notifications to brewery owners, the allowance of additional privileges if law enforcement calls for services and arrests for drunk driving for a specific establishment are nonexistent or low, and alcohol service training for front of house servers. Some of these policies are still in place today, such as server training. This training has been found to assist owners and servers with identifying those who are enjoying the tasting-room experience but not to the point of overservice. This has been very helpful to the industry and the city. See Chapter 10 for more about breweries and crime.

2. Real issue: food trucks needed to stay in a specific location longer

It may seem hard to believe now, but at one time, food trucks were a challenging necessity, and many were called "Roach Coaches." The food trucks of the past served shift workers at numerous manufacturing and office locations during specific work hours each day. These trucks could have potential health and safety issues associated with them, and almost all municipal policies called for food trucks to be at a location for a short period of time, typically 30 minutes and numerous health and safety regulations to keep the public safe. When the breweries requested extended food truck hours at their sites, the city wanted to first understand this change to the food truck industry, so we allowed the food trucks to operate at the breweries in the Business Park for extended hours during a trial period to see if there was a long-term need and, if so, how we should change the codes to meet this new demand. It became apparent very quickly that food trucks (and then catering services) were successful ventures; the types of food trucks showing up at the breweries did not resemble food trucks of the past, and many rivaled "brick and mortar" establishments. The city of Vista, with industry support, changed the city's codes to allow food trucks in the Vista Business Park, as well as after careful review, determined that they should not be allowed in other areas such as the downtown, due to the potential conflict with "brick and mortar" establishments.

There were several other changes that were made to accommodate breweries, which in turn were helping the city with community and economic development. The following three were major changes:

1. Allowed for the issuance of an over-the-counter Minor Use Permit (MUP) for breweries that met several city standard conditions. This was developed in cooperation with the VBG.
2. Implemented catering standards with fewer nonpublic health-related requirements than other municipalities in San Diego County. These included the reduced need for mop basins and washing sinks when brewery facilities were not used for food preparation. Once Vista demonstrated how these lesser requirements could be implemented in a safe and effective manner, several municipalities and San Diego County (for the unincorporated communities) followed suit with similar changes.
3. Allowed for live amplified music inside and outside breweries and tasting rooms. Several code changes were made over time as it became apparent that each industry-supported previous expansion of this use had no substantial negative impacts.

There were also many more minor ones ranging from hours of operation to the provision of expanded outdoor seating.

Moving Forward in Partnership with the Craft Brewing Industry

The ways that cities and the craft brewing industry have and may change in the future and how to respond and support them are questions that continually need to be addressed. Once an industry achieves a certain critical mass, the focus becomes more about stabilizing the industry and less about the number of breweries. Many issues related to helping the industry stabilize are outside of the city's control, but there are a few areas where the city helped and may help in the future. Some of the areas where we can add some light and policy insight are federal, state, and county regulations and even issues related to the private sector.

There is a constant need to think outside of the box. Economic Development staff's job is to look at challenges in a creative way. We work within the system to find solutions that are for the most part a win-win for communities and business owners. If someone thinks it can't be done, economic developers say, "wait a second, let's see how we can do it!" The following are two examples of how we applied this type of thinking in Vista.

1. **Getting beer on BevMo shelves.** Several Vista breweries did not yet have a shelf or store presence, so when BevMo wanted to build a new store in Vista, we got creative. They needed special approval for their use, and during the process of considering the use, we requested that they create a special section for Vista beer and assist those breweries that wanted to get their products into BevMo stores and the BevMo distribution system. To be clear, this was not a requirement of their new location, but since we had a good working relationship with the BevMo team, and we explained the significance of the Vista craft brew community, they were ready to assist. The Vista BevMo created a special section for Vista Craft Beer, and they connected several Vista breweries with their inventory team to help get them into their system for shelf placement and distribution. Win-Win!

2. **Sending beer across the globe.** Economic development looks for opportunities to connect people, companies, products, and solutions. As part of Vista's annual business-support activities, we have a Business Walk where the city and Chamber assemble a team of volunteers to see how our local businesses are doing, again, taking the time to listen. This typically includes 40 volunteers in teams of two that attempt to see a total of 100 businesses in one day. They ask a few questions and let the companies know that we appreciate them being in Vista. During one such occasion, we invited the US Commercial Service's trade specialist in San Diego to participate and assigned her to visit mostly breweries. The trade specialist was so taken by the entrepreneurial attitude and enthusiasm of the breweries that the city and the US Customs Service set up training on how the breweries could export their beer. Within one year, two of our Vista

breweries had exported their beer and had received awards in their new markets for their great products.

Moving Forward

Included here is one final example of how cities and Vista might turn a creative challenge into an opportunity for our craft brewery partners. Carlsbad Raceway operated in the city of Carlsbad at the southern border of Vista for over 40 years, and in 1976, they opened the first commercial skate park in the United States. The raceway and skate park were closed in 2005 due to development, but a group of dedicated fans wanted to commemorate all that happened in this spot from worldwide racing championships to the birth of skateboarding. For almost a decade, the volunteers worked with an adjoining city to locate a monument there, but due to numerous factors, they were unable to do so. The volunteers then found a location in Vista that they thought was perfect. At this specific location, Vista overlooks Oceanside, so they approached Vista city staff with the idea of the Carlsbad Raceway Overlook Monument. Staff took the time to listen and consider how it might support or interfere with surrounding businesses.

Two Vista breweries, Eppig Brewing and Dogleg Brewing, sit right next to the site. The breweries and the property owners of their buildings were supportive of the use as it had potential to bring in additional customers, so the city of Vista approved the monument's placement and construction. Although the monument is yet to be built, it has the potential to support future customers and activities for our local craft beer manufacturers and tasting rooms.

Some questions that remain are: How do we continue to help the industry grow? What are some of those things that will happen in the future that might impact the craft brewers in Vista? What other support might the brewery industry need? These are the types of questions that should be explored in order to be creatively addressed. The story about the Vista craft brew industry is one about a creative group of entrepreneurs who loved their products and wanted to share them with others, but it is also about how the city government, specifically the economic development, can support the emergence of a nascent industry with a little listening and creativity.

12 Designing and Building a Brewery

Zoning and Planning Laws and Restrictions

T. Dustin Hauck

A new craft brewery, as is every other type of development, is governed locally by the zoning and building codes. Zoning codes are hyper-local, specific to the city, town, or county having authority over the property. Building codes are adopted by the state and ratified by each municipality. Zoning codes dictate how a property can be used and what is allowed, sometimes dictating the size, height, appearance, parking, and landscaping of the site. The building code[1] provides the minimum requirements to safeguard public health, safety, and general welfare of the occupants. Both codes are important to understand for a brewery owner as they impact the brewery's development differently.

Every city has its own set municipal rules, often referred to as the municipal code. The codes contain the building blocks for a community, neighborhood, or district. Municipal codes contain zoning code regulations for how land is to be used and the processes required for approvals for development. Planning is the process of creating zoning codes and ensuring development follows the requirements set forth in those codes. The zoning code is the tool that planners use to regulate land use.

Typically, land use regulation is broken down into different plans and ordinances. These may include a General Plan, Specific Plan, community and/or neighborhood plan, zoning ordinances, and sometimes zone-specific regulations meant to spur development in a particular area. The General Plan is a broad description of the community development goals. It is a guide on how land should be used and is the backbone of planning decisions. All other development regulations must follow the rules of the General Plan. A Specific Plan simply implements the General Plan by outlining specific development standards for future development. The community and/or neighborhood plan will focus on a particular area and state policies specific to each community and/or neighborhood. Neighborhoods are then divided into zones, separated into uses, based on the community and/or neighborhood plans.

Why is this important to understand for a craft brewery? A craft brewery is a unique business model where the public is invited to sample and enjoy the product at the same place it is produced or manufactured. The zoning code contains specific regulations on what is allowed in each zone.

DOI: 10.4324/9781003371564-16

Zones are separated into residential, commercial, retail, industrial, agriculture, public infrastructure, utilities, and others. A brewery is considered a "Beer Manufacturing Plant." A taproom can be considered an accessory use to the primary use of manufacturing or may be considered an eating and/or drinking establishment. Every jurisdiction will have its own interpretation. Oftentimes, manufacturing and eating and/or drinking establishments may not be allowed in the same zone. Or they may be allowed with a conditional use permit. There could also be restrictions based on proximity to other zones. An example would be a light commercial zone meant to act as a buffer between a manufacturing zone and a residential zone. Interpreting and understanding what a brewery is and does is critical for the success of getting your brewery permitted. We've seen officials that don't know what a brewery is impart impractical restrictions such as containment basins for cellar tank areas in the event of spill, even though the tanks are non-pressurized, on a wet floor sloped towards a drain, and the product being non-hazardous food grade. We've had to paint over beautiful original brick in a former fire station turned brewery to create a smooth washable surface in a facility where all operations are self-contained, never coming in contact with those surfaces.

Understanding what zones are appropriate for a craft brewery and for a taproom, with or without a kitchen, can dramatically impact what location is right for your operation. If a use permit is required, it is important to understand what that process means, in relation to timeframes, cost, and likelihood of approval.

Zoning codes dictate not only the allowed use of a property but also how that use is permitted. Most codes have provisions for the number of required off-street parking spaces based on how spaces within the building are used. Off-street is the keyword here. Off-street means just that, not including on-street parking that may already be provided in your neighborhood. In the dozens of brewery projects we have worked on, only one time has a city been willing to allow on-street parking to contribute to meeting the off-street parking requirements. These requirements are often based on the use of the building. For example, there may be different required parking ratios for manufacturing, warehouse, office, and customer areas. They are calculated at different ratios depending on how the municipality has outlined it in their code. Some codes are very specific, while others are more general and leave it up to how it is presented and interpretation. To help with excessive parking requirements, some municipalities offer relief based on proximity to public transportation, public parking lots, shared parking agreements with adjacent properties that have more parking than required, or other options. One concept is shared parking based on time of use. Brewing usually starts early in the morning and is often finished well before the taproom opens. The combination of required parking for manufacturing and warehouse use at the same time as the taproom use doesn't always make sense. Those same persons, and their vehicles, are not on site at the same time.

State building codes differ in that they are specifically meant to protect the building occupants' health, safety, and general welfare. The building code protects life safety by limiting the size of a building based on what it is being used for, how it is constructed, and its location on a property. This is important for a brewery and taproom, especially in the redevelopment of an existing building. The requirements for a more populated space, like a taproom, are more restrictive than those for a less populated and more controlled space such as a warehouse or manufacturing facility. In some cases, these limitations can be expanded if the building, for example, is equipped with fire sprinklers or has fire separations between uses. A brewery needs to comply with these regulations in order to be approved by the building department.

Building codes are also responsible for accessibility to, from, and within buildings, ensuring public access for all persons, regardless of their physical abilities. This comes in the form of requirements for access from the public way, parking, accessible paths of travel to the different spaces within the building, and all elements within the building. Building codes have specific requirements for the performance of structural, mechanical, electrical, and plumbing systems.

Building codes also dictate how much lot coverage can occur, number of stories, building height, percentage of landscaping required, ingress and egress of the site by the public, signage, and even the materials used, all of which can impact the planning, layout, construction, and operation of your brewery.

When a building undergoes a change of use, meaning it is changing from the use it was originally intended for to a new and different use, that triggers bringing the building up to the current codes. This can entail upgrading parking, accessible paths from the public right-of-way to the building entrance and throughout the building, ADA improvements to restroom facilities, and even public improvements. We recently completed a project for a small brewery that needed to relocate due to its lease expiring at a different location. The new space they chose was a former warehouse that had not been used as a manufacturing facility. This change of use not only triggered the items mentioned earlier but also required improvements in the public right-of-way such as replacement of city sidewalks and additional street trees. We've even seen the impacts of the pandemic during the design of a project drastically impact the scope and timeline for a project. On the rare occasion, we get lucky with a municipality that really pushes for and assists breweries (see Chapter 11 for an example of this). We've seen incentives such as free expedited plan checks or even discounted to zero cost permit fees. Zoning departments are able to interpret their own codes and regulations in beneficial ways to help spawn development. However, the building department is not the same. The health and safety of the public must be the primary concern.

Zoning codes and building codes that govern a specific jurisdiction can have a dramatic impact on the design of a brewery for all the reasons stated earlier. A craft brewery is unique; it is a blend of manufacturing and hospitality uses. A brewery could be interpreted as a commercial space, a retail space, an industrial space, and even an agricultural space; the mixing of which is not commonly accounted for in most zoning and building codes. Understanding how the local authorities having jurisdiction over the project think and interpret the code will help navigate the approval process. This will help understand what zones and properties may be better suited for a craft brewery, facilitating less costly and more timely development.

As the popularity of craft breweries expand, many municipalities have recognized this disparity and have begun to incorporate specific provisions in their zoning codes for breweries. Perhaps they are treated like a bakery, allowed in a residential or adjacent commercial zone, seen as a critical amenity for the community. A brewery is different from a typical bar or pub. They are oftentimes a gathering place for the community, a place for persons of all ages, families included. Craft breweries often attract different clientele, focusing on quality over quantity, committed to the neighborhood. For this reason, they are usually regulated differently from a bar or pub. Patrons tend to spend a few hours or less, consuming less alcohol, while the business often closes early as families head home.

Craft breweries can benefit a community by encouraging other developments nearby, often with its influx of interest to the neighborhood. Adaptive reuse of underutilized or underperforming properties and neighborhoods can spur growth. They contribute to development by spurring complimentary business such as restaurants, art galleries, and other artisan producers.

There have been numerous case studies proving how a craft brewery has spawned activity in an area, oftentimes repurposing older buildings, hinting at the past and our history, while bringing new life without demolition of an existing structure (see more on this in Chapter 2). These case studies are opportunities for cities, towns, and counties to learn how to encourage growth and reduce or eliminate barriers to entry for breweries. But these case studies alone are not enough. Planners need to understand the needs and desires of a brewery operator as much as that operator needs to understand their municipality. Zoning codes can be more inclusive to development in zones once not thought appropriate for hospitality uses. They can be more open to mixed uses, taking into consideration how a brewery operates, what its needs are, and how those needs weave into the integration with the tasting room experience.

When building a brewery, there are several high barriers to entry that are important to consider.

1. Long permit processes, often taking over six to eight months for approval, not to mention a special use permit, which doubles or triples that time. A tenant usually needs to have a lease in place to start the review process. This can involve paying rent for many months while a determination is made, without knowing if the project will be approved or viable after conditions are determined. One way that cities can reduce that timeframe is by offering concurrent processing of building and use permits. This would allow for an expedited process, not waiting for one to be approved to proceed with the other. The long timelines for approvals make it difficult to secure a location due to the added carrying cost.

2. A landlord might not be as amenable to not knowing for months if a tenant will be able to get approval to continue with a project. Landlords can also be reluctant to allow the destructive improvements that are necessary for a brewery. Removal of existing floors to accommodate sloping toward new drains may be more than what a landlord will want to allow.

3. High utility demand of electrical, natural gas, water, and sewer systems can also be barriers to entry. Many warehouse and retail locations are not equipped with the utilities a brewery needs. This requires expensive upgrades to those systems, sometimes not even possible. If you need more electrical service, is that added capacity available from the utility company? If you need natural gas and it is not already to the building, is that even available nearby?

4. Environmental concerns such as hazardous materials, wastewater, stormwater, odor, and noise just add to the list of barriers for a brewery operator to overcome.

There is a lot to think about and try to plan for when deciding to open a craft brewery. We've seen a wide variety of non-typical brewery development. These include: trying to construct a brewery in a historic building along a potential railway path; adapting to a municipal code that has no provisions for a brewery or allowing a mix of manufacturing and a taproom in the same building; extraordinarily long and arduous building and use permit timelines; complicated existing buildings that were not designed to ever house a brewery such as multi-story mixed-use building with parking garages below and residential uses above; converting a turn of the century, dilapidated, historic church into a taproom; and dealing with seismic faults that cross the project property. All of these create unique situations that must be factored in the cost, time, and effort of the project.

My advice for anyone looking to start or expand a brewery is to hire someone that has experience and knows what to look for, or just where to look. Sometimes where you look is just as good as knowing what you are looking for. Research the process with your city! Find out what permits will be required and what the cost and timeline look like to obtain them. Know what utilities your brewery needs and what it is going to take to upgrade them if necessary. Understand what you are good at (brewing beer!) and bring in the people you need to do what you can't or don't have the time or expertise.

Note

1 International Code Council, 2018, International Building Code, "Effective Use of the International Building Code."

References

Alaska Electric Light and Power Company. (2016). *Tunnel & lake tap*. www.aelp.com/About-Us/annex-creek-project/tunnel-and-lake-tap

Alaskan Brewing Company. *Beer powdered beer*. www.alaskanbeer.com/beerpoweredbeer/

Alexander, D. (2013, November 26). Beer entrepreneurs fuel comeback of struggling Cleveland neighborhood. *Forbes*. www.forbes.com/sites/danalexander/2013/11/26/beer-entrepreneurs-fuel-comeback-of-struggling-cleveland-neighborhood/#191d718312ca

Amoriello, T., Mellara, F., Galli, V., Amoriello, M., & Ciccoritti, R. (2020). Technological properties and consumer acceptability of bakery products enriched with brewers' spent grains. *Food*, *9*(10), 1492. https://doi.org/10.3390/foods9101492

Anderson Economic Group, LLC. (2019). *The economic impact of beer tourism in Kent county*. Experience Grand Rapids.

Andrea Belmartino & Natacha Liseras. (2020). The Craft Beer Market in Argentina: An Exploratory Study of Local Brewers' and Consumers' Perceptions in Mar del Plata, *Papers in Applied Geography*, *6*(3), 190–203. DOI: 10.1080/23754931.2020.1747525

Apardian, R. E., Nilsson, I., Reid, N., & Wartell, J. (2022). The role of neighborhood characteristics for firm performance in the experience economy: A case study of production volumes in California's brewpub industry. *Journal of Urban Management*, *11*(2), 214–225. https://doi.org/10.1016/j.jum.2022.05.010

Apardian, R. E., & Reid, N. (2020). Going out for a pint: Exploring the relationship between craft brewery locations and neighborhood walkability. *Papers in Applied Geography*, *6*(3), 240–255. https://doi.org/10.1080/23754931.2019.1699151

Atkinson, R. (2003). Domestication by cappuccino or a revenge on urban space? Control and empowerment in the management of public spaces. *Urban Studies*, *40*(9), 1829–1843.

Atkinson, R., & Bridge, G. (Eds.) (2005). *Gentrification in a Global Context: The New Urban Colonialism*. London: Routledge.

Autor, D. (2022, March 14). The shrinking share of middle-income jobs. *Econofact*. https://econofact.org/the-shrinking-share-of-middle-income-jobs

Backus, L. (2019, September 24). CT brewery bans kids and pets. *The Middletown Press*. www.middletownpress.com/middletown/article/CT-brewery-bans-kids-and-pets-14463196.php

Baginski, J., & Bell, T. L. (2011). Under-tapped? An analysis of craft brewing in the Southern United States. *Southeastern geographer*, *51*(1), 165–185.

Barajas, J., Boeing, G., & Wartell, J. (2017). Neighborhood change, one pint at a time: The impact of local characteristics on craft breweries. In *Untapped: Exploring the cultural dimensions of craft beer* (pp. 155–176). West Virginia University Press.

Bates, Lisa K. (2013). Gentrification and Displacement Study: Implementing an Equitable Inclusive Development Strategy in the Context of Gentrification. *Urban Studies and Planning Faculty Publications and Presentations.* https://doi.org/10.15760/report-01

Bartlett, D., Allen, S., Harris, J., & Cary, L. (2013). Revitalization One Pint at a Time: How Breweries and Distilleries Contribute to Main Street. In *Oregon Main Street Conference, Astoria, OR*, October (pp. 2–4).

Battisto, J., de Zeeuw, M., Landau, R., Misera, L., Sánchez, A., Wiersch, A. M., & Williams, J. (2022). *Small business credit survey: 2021 Report on firms owned by people of color.* U.S. Federal Reserve System.

Bcorporation.net. (2023). *B impact assessment.* www.bcorporation.net/en-us/programs-and-tools/b-impact-assessment

Becker, D. (2009, May 13). Alaskan brewing – a new release and brewhouse innovation. *The Full Pint: Craft Beer News.* https://thefullpint.com/beer-news/alaskan-brewing-a-new-release-and-brewhouse-innovation/

Becker, D. (2022, July 18). Stone brewing promotes from within ahead of major expansion. *The Full Pint: Craft Beer News.* https://thefullpint.com/beer-news/stone-brewing-promotes-from-within-ahead-of-major-expansion/

Becker, D. (2022, March 3). Stone brewing announces expansion of Richmond, VA production. *The Full Pint: Craft Beer News.* https://thefullpint.com/beer-news/stone-brewing-announces-expansion-of-richmond-va-production/

BeerInfo. (2020, April 29). *Brewing schools in the United States.* https://beerinfo.com/brewing-schools-in-the-united-states/

Berhman, J. (2001, April 10). Stone brewing drops restaurant plans. *The San Diego Union-Tribune.* www.sandiegouniontribune.com/sdut-stone-brewing-restaurant-wins-planners-approval-2001mar06-story.html

Beverage Industry Environmental Roundtable. (2022, January). *beverage industry continues to drive improvement in water, energy, and emissions efficiency: 2021 Water and energy use benchmarking study.* www.bieroundtable.com/publication/2021-water-and-energy-use-benchmarking-study/

Bivens, J. (2019, January 23). Updated employment multipliers for the U.S. economy. *Economic Policy Institute.* www.epi.org/publication/updated-employment-multipliers-for-the-u-s-economy/

Bizinelli, C., Manosso, F. C., Gândara, J., & Valduga, V. (2013). Beer tourism experiences in Curitiba, PR. *Rosa dos Ventos, 5*(2), 349–375. www.cabdirect.org/cabdirect/abstract/20133405220

Bobonick, E. (2022, June 7). New wave of Cincinnati breweries take a lesson from the past to find recipes for success. *Soapbox.* www.soapboxmedia.com/features/new-wave-breweries-first-suburbs.aspx

Bock, K. (2015). The changing nature of city tourism and its possible implications for the future of cities. *European Journal of Futures Research, 3*(20). https://doi.org/10.1007/s40309-015-0078-5

Bolet, D. (2021). Drinking alone: Local socio-cultural degradation and radical right support – the case of British pub closures. *Comparative Political Studies, 54*(9), 1653–1692. https://doi.org/10.1177/0010414021997158

Bourdieu, P. (1984). *A social critique of the judgement of taste.* Traducido del francés por R. Nice. Londres, Routledge.

Brantingham, P., & Brantingham, P. (1995). Criminality of place: Crime generators and crime attractors. *European Journal on Criminal Policy and Research, 13,* 5–26.

Brewers Association. (2021, February 9). Brewers association sustainability manuals. *Brewers Association.* www.brewersassociation.org/brewing-industry-updates/sustainability-manuals/

Brewers Association. (2022, October 7). Brewery production stats and data. *Brewers Association.* www.brewersassociation.org/statistics-and-data/brewery-production-data/

Brewers' Law. (2022). *Common zoning challenges for Florida beverage manufacturers.* https://brewerslaw.com/common-zoning-challenges-for-fl-beverage-manufacturers/

Brewery Vivant. (2022, November 8). *About.* https://breweryvivant.com/about

Broken Cauldron. (2015). "Staff Report to the Municipal Planning Board" for the City of Orlando – http://www.cityoforlando.net/greenworks/wp-content/uploads/sites/27/2015/07/MPBStaffReport2015-07_CUP2015-00008.pdf

Brooks, J. R. (2013). *California breweries north.* Stackpole Books.

Brown-Saracino, Japonica. (2010). *A Neighborhood That Never Changes: Gentrification, Social Preservation, and the Search for Authenticity.* University of Chicago Press. Chicago Scholarship Online, 2013. https://doi.org/10.7208/chicago/9780226076645.001.0001.

Buechler, J., Rhenish, M., Miles, W., Fusco, A., & Ellis, R. (2016, June 1) *Ask the expert: Barreling ahead. What happens when microbrews go macro?* Harvard Business School.

Bullen, P. A. (2007). Adaptive reuse and sustainability of commercial buildings. *Facilities, 25*(1–2), 20–31. https://doi.org/10.1108/02632770710716911

Bullen, P. A., & Love, P. E. D. (2011). Adaptive reuse of heritage buildings. *Structural Survey, 29*(5), 411–421.

Burgdorf, J. E. (2016). Essays on mandated vertical restraints. *All Dissertations, 1659.* https://tigerprints.clemson.edu/all_dissertations/1659

Burrowes, J., Young, A., Restuccia, D., Fuller, J., & Raman, M. (2014, November). *Bridge the gap: Rebuilding America's middle skills.* Harvard Business School.

Cabras, I. (2021). Craft beers and breweries in the United Kingdom: Where now, what next? In *Case studies in the beer sector* (pp. 37–48). Woodhead Publishing.

Cabras, I., Lorusso, M., & Waehning, N. (2020). Measuring the economic contribution of beer festivals on local economies: The case of York, United Kingdom. *International Journal of Tourism Research, 22*(6), 739–750. https://doi.org/10.1002/jtr.2369

California Community Colleges Chancellor's Office. (2022). *Prestigious certification helps Miracosta's Brewtech program turn craft beers into careers.* www.cccco.edu/About-Us/News-and-Media/California-Community-Colleges-Outlook-Newsletter/craft-brew-to-careers

California State University San Marcos. (2022, November 4). *EngiBeering certificate.* www.csusm.edu/el/programs/science-technology/certengibeering/index.html

Campbell, C. A., Hahn, R. A., Elder, R., Brewer, R., Chattopadhyay, S., Fielding, J., Naimi, T. S., Toomey, T., Lawrence, B., & Middleton, J. C. (2009). The effectiveness of limiting alcohol outlet density as a means of reducing excessive alcohol consumption and alcohol-related harms. *American Journal of Preventive Medicine, 37*(6), 556–69. https://doi.org/10.1016/j.amepre.2009.09.028

Canadian Craft Brewers Association. (2023, January 9). *The voice of Canadian craft beer*. https://ccba-ambc.org/

The Canadian Encyclopedia. (2017, March 14). *Industrialization in Canada*. www.the-canadianencyclopedia.ca/en/article/industrialization

Carley, S., & Yahng, L. (2018). Willingness-to-pay for sustainable beer. *PLoS One, 13*(10). https://doi.org/10.1371/journal.pone.0204917

CBRE Research. (2016, January). Ohio craft beer . . . taking flight. *CBRE*. https://cbree mail.com/cv/4d16a7f80cabe5342d7379bee8fb517b0332dc72

Chapman, N., & Brunsma, D. (2020). *Beer and racism: How beer became white, why it matters, and the movements to change it* (pp. 131–154). Bristol University Press. doi:10.46692/9781529201765.008

Cheung, K. (2019, August 28). Cheers to locally sourced beer. *Black Swan Data*. www.blackswan.com/cheers-to-locally-sourced-beer/

Chirakranont, R., & Sunanta, S. (2021). Applications of experience economy in craft beer tourism: A case study in Thailand's context. *Sustainability, 13*(18), 10448. https://doi.org/10.3390/su131810448

Chitwood, K. (2019, February 12). Brewery church' is the latest in craft of luring folks to church. *Religion News Service*. https://religionnews.com/2019/02/12/brewery-church-is-the-latest-in-craft-of-luring-folks-to-church/

Chorna, I. (2022, June 21). Skills-based hiring: Why traditional hiring methods don't work anymore. *HRForecast*. https://hrforecast.com/the-rise-of-skills-based-hiring-or-why-your-old-hiring-approach-doesnt-work-anymore/

Chung, J., (2008, July 20). Hard for Brooklyn Brewery to Find a New Brooklyn Home. Gothamist.com. http://gothamist.com/2008/07/20/hard_for_brooklyn_brewery_to_find_a.php

Church Brew Works. (2022). *History*. https://churchbrew.com/history/

Clark, D. (2008, April 1). Adapting an older building for a new use. *Buildings*. www.buildings.com/articles/34689/adapting-older-building-new-use

Clarke, R. V. (1980). "Situational" crime prevention: Theory and practice. *The British Journal of Criminology, 20*(2), 136–147. https://doi.org/10.1093/oxfordjournals.bjc.a047153

Clarke, R. V. (1995). Situational crime prevention. *Crime and Justice, 19*, 91–150.

Clifford, C. (2017, May 4). How America's no. 1 small business got to $10 million brewing beer in Hawaii. *CNBC*. www.cnbc.com/2017/05/04/americas-no-1-small-business-got-to-10-million-brewing-beer.html

Climate Neutral. (2022). *Pure project: A climate neutral certified brand*. www.climate-neutral.org/brand/pure-project

Cohen, L. E., & Felson, M. (1979). Social change and crime rate trends: A routine activity approach. *American Sociological Review, 44*, 588–608. http://dx.doi.org/10.2307/2094589

Colicchio, P., Schneck, T., Flora, P., Copenhaver, C., & Reiff, K. (2019). Something's brewing in CRE. *The Edge Magazine, 2*, 48–52.

Colliers International. (2020, April 5). *Craft beer pours into commercial real estate*. United States Documents. https://documents.pub/document/craft-beer-pours-into-commercial-real-estate-contract-brewing-company-a-business.html

Concepcion, M. (2019, August 13). c. *San Diego business journal*. sdbj.com/finance/economy/san-diego-countys-craft-brewers-produce-12-billion/

Contreras, D. R. (2019). *San Diego beer industry timeline*. City of San Diego Economic Development Department.

Cornish, D., & Clarke, R. V. (1986). *The reasoning criminal: Rational choice perspectives on offending. Hague.* Springer- Verlag.

Cornish, D., & Clarke, R. V. (2003). Opportunities, precipitators and criminal decisions: A reply to Wortley's critique of situational crime prevention. *Crime Prevention Studies, 16*, 41–96.

Cortright, J. (2002). The Economic Importance of Being Different: Regional Variations in Tastes, Increasing Returns, and the Dynamics of Development. *Economic Development Quarterly, 16*(1), 3–16. https://doi.org/10.1177/0891242402016001001

Cozens, P., & Grieve, S. (2014). Situational crime prevention at nightclub entrances in Perth, Western Australia: Exploring micro-level crime precipitators. *Crime Prev Community Safety, 16*(1), 54–70. https://doi.org/10.1057/cpcs.2013.14

Crociata, A. (2020). The Role of Cultural Capital in Beer Consumption in Italy: An Exploratory Study, *Papers in Applied Geography, 6*(3), 180–189, DOI: 10.1080/23754931.2020.1741431

Crouch, A. (2018, September). Of tykes and taprooms: Do kids belong in breweries? *Beer Advocate.* www.beeradvocate.com/articles/17500/of-tykes-and-taprooms-do-kids-belong-in-breweries

Crowell, C. (2018, July 17). Anaheim craft brewer incentives pay off as city touts growing craft beer scene. *Craft Brewing Business.* www.craftbrewingbusiness.com/news/anaheim-craft-brewer-incentives-pay-off-as-city-touts-growing-craft-beer-scene/

Cushman & Wakefield. (2017, June). *Craft brew: The craft brewing revolution.* https://cushwake.cld.bz/CW-Retail-Craft-Brew-Report/1

Dense, J. (2020). Economic impact of craft beer festivals. In N. Hoalst-Pullen & M. Patterson (Eds.), *The geography of beer*. Springer.

Duff, J. (2018, April 18). *Brewed in heritage*. National Trust for Canada. https://nationaltrustcanada.ca/online-stories/brewed-in-heritage

Dunbar, R. I. M., Launay, J., Wlodarski, R., Robertson, C., Pearce, E., Carney, J., & MacCarron, P. (2017). Functional benefits of (Modest) alcohol consumption. *Adaptive Human Behavior and Physiology, 3*(2), 118–133. https://doi.org/10.1007/s40750-016-0058-4

Eberts, D. (2014). Neolocalism and the branding and marketing of place by Canadian microbreweries. *The geography of beer: Regions, environment, and societies*, 189–199.

Eck, J. E., Clarke, R. V., & Guerette, R. T. (2007). Risky facilities: Crime concentration in homogeneous sets of establishments and facilities. *Crime Prevention Studies, 21*, 225–264.

Eco-Friendly Beer Drinker. (2020, April 20). These certified B Corp breweries value people and planet as much as profits. *Eco Friendly Beer.* https://ecofriendlybeer.com/a-toast-to-the-b-corp-breweries-putting-employees-environment-and-community-on-par-with-profits/

Elder, A. (2010, March 16). The craft beer capital of America. *San Diego Magazine.* www.sandiego.org/campaigns/good-stuff/craft-beer.aspx

Elkington, J. (2013). *Enter the triple bottom line*. Routledge.

Fairlie, R. W., & Robb, A. M. (2010). *Disparities in capital access between minority and non-minority-owned businesses*. U.S. Department of Commerce.

Fauble, L. (2019, October 16). Maui brewing goes off-the-grid. *Craftbeer.com.* www. craftbeer.com/featured-brewery/maui-brewing-goes-off-the-grid

Feeney, A. E. (2017a). Beer-trail maps and the growth of experiential tourism. *Cartographic Perspectives, 87*, 9–28. https://doi.org/10.14714/CP87.1383

Feeney, A. E. (2017b). Cultural heritage, sustainable development, and the impacts of craft breweries in Pennsylvania. *City, Culture and Society, 9*, 21–30. https://doi.org/10.1016/j.ccs.2017.03.001

Finlay, J., Esposito, M., Kim, M. H., Gomez-Lopez, I., & Clarke, P. (2019). Closure of 'third places'? Exploring potential consequences for collective health and wellbeing. *Health & Place, 60*, 102225. https://doi.org/10.1016/j.healthplace.2019.102225

First Insight, Inc, The Baker Retailing Center at Wharton School of the University of Pennsylvania. (2021, November). *The state of consumer spending – Gen Z influencing all generations to make sustainability-first purchasing decisions.*

Flack, W. (1997). American microbreweries and neolocalism: "Ale-ing" for a sense of place. *Journal of Cultural Geography, 16*(2), 37–53. https://doi.org/10.1080/08873639709478336

Fletchall, A. M. (2016). Place-making through beer-drinking: A case study of Montana's craft breweries. *Geographical Review, 106*(4), 539–566. https://doi.org/10.1111/j.1931-0846.2016.12184.x

Florida, R. (2003). Cities and the Creative Class. *City & Community, 2*(1), 3–19. https://doi.org/10.1111/1540-6040.00034

Florida, R. (2017, August 15). Can Craft Breweries Transform America's Post-Industrial Neighborhoods? *Bloomberg.Com.* https://www.bloomberg.com/news/articles/2017-08-15/craft-beer-is-transforming-post-industrial-neighborhoods

Forbes, D. (2014, March 11). BeerCity USA poll retires, 'served its purpose'. *Mountain Express.* https://mountainx.com/blogwire/beercity_usa_poll_retires_served_its_purpose/

Foust, J. (2016, July 25). New Belgium brewing company earns platinum certification. *U.S. Zero Waste Business Council.* https://dpw.lacounty.gov/epd/SBR/pdfs/ZeroWasteNewBelgium.pdf

Fuller, J. B., Langer, C., Nitschke, J., O'Kane, L., Sigelman, M., & Taska, B. (2022). *The emerging degree reset: How the shift to skills-based hiring holds the keys to growing the U.S. Workforce at a time of talent shortage.* The Burning Glass Institute.

Fuller, J. B., & Raman, M. (2017). *Dismissed by degrees: How degree inflation is undermining U.S. competitiveness and hurting America's middle class.* Harvard Business School.

Garavaglia, C. (2020). The emergence of Italian craft breweries and the development of their local identity. In N. Hoalst-Pullen & M. Patterson (Eds.), *The geography of beer.* Springer.

García Lamarca, M. (2020, March 20). *How one of Montréal's poorest neighborhoods became ripe for green gentrification.* Barcelona Laboratory for Urban Environmental Justice and Sustainability. www.bcnuej.org/2020/03/24/how-one-of-montreals-poorest-neighborhoods-became-ripe-for-green-gentrification/

Gatrell, J. D., Reid, N., & Steiger, T. L. (2018). Branding spaces: Place, region, sustainability and the American craft beer industry. *Applied Geography, 90*, 360–370. https://doi.org/10.1016/j.apgeog.2017.02.012

Gerrard, J. (2018, March 12). New Belgium earns platinum certification for zero waste initiatives. *Food Engineering.* www.foodengineeringmag.com/articles/95985-new -belgium-earns-platinum-certification-for-zero-waste-initiatives

Gibbon, R. (2005). *City of San Diego annual report of the business expansion attraction & retention team.* City of San Diego Economic Development Department.

Gibbons, J., & Barton, M. (2016). The association of minority self-related health with black versus white gentrification. *Journal of Urban Health: Bulletin of the New York Academy of Medicin, 93*(6), 909–922. doi: 10.1007/s11524-016-0087-0.

Giedeman, D., Isely, P., & Simons, G. (2015). *The economic impact of beer tourism in Kent County, Michigan.* https://assets.simpleviewcms.com/simpleview/image/up load/v1/clients/grandrapids/BeerTourismReportOctober2015_fbe5aa4a-bb4f-42ad-b86f-c6ca88f0ae1f.pdf

Gorski, E. (2015). Denver's river north neighborhood: The brewing district. *The Denver Post.* www.denverpost.com/2015/02/16/denvers-river-north-neighborhood-the-brewing-district

Graham, K. (2009). They fight because we let them! Applying a situational crime prevention model to barroom violence. *Drug and Alcohol Review, 28*, 103–109. https://doi.org/10.1111/j.1465-3362.2008.00038.x

Graham, K., & Homel, R. (2008). *Raising the bar: Preventing aggression in and around bars, pubs and clubs.* Willan Publishing.

Gruenewald, P. J. (2007). The spatial ecology of alcohol problems: Niche theory and assortative drinking. *Addiction, 102*(6), 870–878. https://doi.org/10.1111/j.1360-0443.2007.01856.x

Grunde, J., Siqi, L., & Merl, R. (2014). Craft breweries and sustainability: Challenges, solutions, and positive impacts. *DIVA.* www.diva-portal.org/smash/record.jsf?pid=d iva2%3A829201&dswid=114

Gustafson, C. (2005, April 27). *Stone brewery takes a few hops – business park's first tenant moving from San Marcos.* The San Diego Union-Tribune.

Ham, A., Maldonado, D., Weintraub, M., Camacho, A. F., & Gualtero, D. (2022). Reducing alcohol-related violence with bartenders: A behavioral field experiment. *Journal of Policy Analysis and Management, 41*, 731–761. https://doi.org/10.1002/pam.22365

Hancock, C., Sewake, G., & Donovan, M. (2018). *Craft breweries and community.* University of New Hampshire Cooperative Extension. https://scholars.unh.edu/cgi/viewcontent.cgi?article=2202&context=extension

Healey, P. (1998). Building institutional capacity through collaborative approaches to urban planning. *Environment and Planning A: Economy and Space, 30*(9), 1531–1546. https://doi.org/10.1068/a301531

Hermann, U. P., Boshoff, L., & Ncala, T. T. (2019). Understanding beer festival attendee motivations to a craft beer festival in South Africa. *Journal for New Generation Sciences, 17*(2), 18–30.

Hernandez, B. (2014, December 3). Stone brewing Richmond. *Stone Brewing Blog.* www.stonebrewing.com/blog/venues/2014/stone-brewing-richmond

Holl, J. (2018, May 9). Addressing the question: Are kids welcome in breweries? *Craft Beer & Brewing.* https://beerandbrewing.com/addressing-the-question-are-kids-welcome-in-breweries/

Holtkamp, C., Shelton, T., Daly, G., Hiner, C. C., & Hagelman III, R. R. (2016). Assessing neolocalism in microbreweries. *Papers in Applied Geography, 2*(1), 66–78. https://doi.org/10.1080/23754931.2015.1114514

Hughes, C. J. (2018, February 27). How craft breweries are helping to revive local economies. *The New York Times*. www.nytimes.com/2018/02/27/business/craft-breweries-local-economy.html

Infante, D. (2020, July 28). Gentrivitalization by brewery. *Fingers*. www.fingers.email/p/gentrivitalization-by-brewery

Infanzon, V. (2019, January 24). NoDa's charm is like a 'quirky mayberry' – neighborhood stories. *Charlotte Stories*. www.charlottestories.com/noda-neighborhood-stories/

International Code Council, Inc. (2018). *Effective use of the international building code*. International Code Council, Inc.

İsildar, P., & Yildiz, O. E. (2020). Izmir craft beer trail. *Universal Journal of Management, 8*(4), 209–219. https://doi.org/10.13189/ujm.2020.080501

Jackson-Beckham, J. N. (2019). *Diversity and inclusion for small and independent craft breweries: Assessing your efforts*. Brewers Association.

Jasch, C. (2000). Environmental performance evaluation and indicators. *Journal of Cleaner Production, 8*(1), 79–88. https://doi.org/10.1016/s0959-6526(99)00235-8

Jolly, C., Settle, Q., & Greenhaw, L. (2021). Community stakeholders' perspectives of craft breweries in their communities in Oklahoma. *Journal of Applied Communications, 105*(4), 1–7. https://doi.org/10.4148/1051-0834.2383

Kaplan, S. M. (2018, June 18). *A look back: San Diego beer history from 1868–1953*. San Diego Westcoaster. https://archives.csusm.edu/westcoastersd/2018/09/13/a-look-back-san-diego-beer-history-from-1868-to-1953/

Kearns, G., & Philo, C. (Eds.). (1993). *Selling places: the city as cultural capital, past and present*. Pergamon.

Khan, A. (2021, April 27). Alberta craft brewer gets funding for carbon recycling system. *Sustainable Biz Canada*. https://sustainablebiz.ca/blindman-brewery-craft-fund-carbon-recycling/

Kickert, C. (2021). What's in store: Prospects and challenges for American street-level commerce. *Journal of Urban Design, 26*(2), 159–177. https://doi.org/10.1080/1357 4809.2019.1686352

Kim, G. (2016). The Public Value of Urban Vacant Land: Social Responses and Ecological Value. *Sustainability, 8*(5), 486. https://doi.org/10.3390/su8050486

Kirby, J., & Lundy, M. (2022, April 21). Canada's crowded craft beer industry is tapped out. What brewers say must happen to Stayy Afloat. *The Globe and Mail*. www.theglobeandmail.com/business/article-canada-craft-beer-industry-covid-oversaturated-market/

Kiss, T. (2015, May 17). Saving local history with . . . beer? Breweries give old buildings new life. *Greenville News*. www.greenvilleonline.com/story/money/business/2015/05/17/breweries-historic-buildings/27307697/

Klobucista, C., & Robinson, K. (2021, April 22). Water stress: A global problem that's getting worse. *Council on Foreign Relations*. www.cfr.org/backgrounder/water-stress-global-problem-thats-getting-worse

Koch, G. (2019, April 5). Stone brewing berlin: Too big, too bold, too soon. *Stone Brewing Blog*. www.stonebrewing.com/blog/venues/2019/farewell-stone-brewing-berlin

Kovach, E. (2020, March 4). The who behind the brew: Tess Hart of triple bottom brewing. *PA Eats*. www.paeats.org/feature/triple-bottom-brewing/

Kraftchick, J., Byrd, E., Canziani, B., & Gladwell, N. (2014). Understanding beer tourist motivation. *Tourism Management Perspectives, 12,* 41–47. https://doi.org/10.1016/j. tmp.2014.07.001

Laska, S. B., & Spain, D. (1980). Anticipating Renovators' Demands: New Orleans. In *Back to the City,* (pp. 116–137). Pergamon.

Lehnert, M., Nilsson, I., & Reid, N. (2020). Navigating the regulatory environment in American urban areas: The case of craft breweries. In E. S. Madsen, J. Gammelgaard, & B. Hobdari (Eds.), *New developments in the brewing industry: The role of institutions and ownerships.* Oxford University Press.

Lewin, S. S., & Goodman, C. (2013). Transformative renewal and urban sustainability. *Journal of Green Building, 8*(4), 17–38. https://doi.org/10.3992/jgb.8.4.17

Lipton, R., Yang, X., Braga, A. A., Goldstick, J., Newton, M., & Rura, M. (2013). The geography of violence, alcohol outlets, and drug arrests in Boston. *American Journal of Public Health, 103*(4), 657–664. https://doi.org/10.2105/AJPH.2012.300927

Livingston, M. (2011). Alcohol outlet density and harm: Comparing the impacts on violence and chronic harms. *Drug and Alcohol Review, 30*(5), 515–523. https://doi. org/10.1111/j.1465-3362.2010.00251.x

Logan, J. R., & Molotch, H. L. (1987). *Urban Fortunes: The Political Economy of Place.* University of California Press. http://www.gbv.de/dms/bowker/toc/9780520063419.pdf

Lynch, N. (2021). Remaking the obsolete: Critical geographies of contemporary adaptive reuse. *Geography Compass, 16*(1). https://doi.org/10.1111/gec3.12605

Madensen, T. D., & Eck, J. E. (2008). Violence in bars: Exploring the impact of place manager decision-making. *Crime Prevention and Community Safety, 10*(2), 111–125. https://doi.org/10.1057/cpcs.2008.2

Mapp, L. (2023, January 21). In *unprecedented move, Rincon withdraws from California tribal gaming compact.* San Diego Union-Tribune. https://www.sandiegouniontribune. com/entertainment/casinos/story/2023-01-21/in-unprecedented-news-rincon-withdraws-from-california-tribal-gaming-compact

Mars, R., & Kohlstedt, K. (2020). *The 99% invisible city: A field guide to the hidden world of everyday design.* Houghton.

Mathews, V. (2020, February 27). *Telling the stories of place through craft beer.* Department of Geography & Environmental Studies, University of Regina. https:// heritagesask.ca/pub/events/Heritage%20Forum%202020/Dr.%20Vanessa%20 Mathews%20-%20Telling%20the%20Stories%20of%20Place%20through%20 Craft%20Beer.pdf

Mathews, V., & Picton, R. M. (2014). Intoxifying gentrification: Brew pubs and the geography of post-industrial heritage. *Urban Geography, 35*(3), 337–356. https:// doi.org/10.1080/02723638.2014.887298

Mathews, V., & Picton, R. M. (2023). Craft breweries as hermit crabs: Adaptive reuse and the revaluation of place. *Local Development & Society.* https://doi.org/10.1080/ 26883597.2022.2163918

Maui Brewing Company. (2019, September 27). *Maui brewing company reaches completion of its renewable energy project.* https://mauibrewingco.com/press/maui-brewing-company-reaches-completion-of-its-renewable-energy-project/

McCullough, M. P., Berning, J., & Hanson, J. L. (2018). Learn by Brewing: Homebrewing legalization and the brewing industry. *Contemporary Economic Policy, 37*(5). https://doi.org/10.1111/coep.12394

McKean, J. (2010, February 1). Our gardens receive shiny stamp of professional approval. *Stone Brewing Blog*. www.stonebrewing.com/blog/miscellany/2010/our-gardens-receive-shiny-stamp-professional-approval

McKean, J. (2011, September 12). Community supported agriculture: Stone's next frontier. *Stone Brewing Blog*. www.stonebrewing.com/blog/philosophy/2011/community-supported-agriculture-stone's-next-frontier

Mehr, S. Y., & Wilkinson, S. (2020). The importance of place and authenticity in adaptive reuse of heritage buildings. *International Journal of Building Pathology and Adaptation, 38*(5), 689–701. https://doi.org/10.1108/IJBPA-01-2020-0005

Mercer, J. (2014, September 19). Wastewater basics for a growing craft brewery. *Craft Brewing Business*. www.craftbrewingbusiness.com/equipment-systems/wastewater-basics-growing-craft-brewery

Mirabella, L. (2018, September 13). In controversial move, union craft brewing bans children after 6 p.m. *The Baltimore Sun*. www.baltimoresun.com/food-drink/bs-bz-union-craft-brewing-children-ban-20180912-story.html

MiraCosta College. (2022). *CE0006 craft brewing technician (Brewtech) certificate*. Community Education & Workforce Development. https://commed.mira costa.edu/public/category/courseCategoryCertificateProfile.do?method=load&c ertificateId=1142647&selectedProgramAreaId=1016641&selectedProgramStrea mId=1016667

Moore, M. S., Reid, N., & McLaughlin, R. B. (2016). The locational determinants of micro-breweries and Brewpubs in the United States. In I. Cabras, D. Higgins, & D. Preece (Eds.), *Brewing, beer and pubs*. Palgrave Macmillan.

Morales, I. (2022, January 24). Social entrepreneurship with triple bottom brewing company. *Yale School of Management*. https://som.yale.edu/story/2022/social-entrepreneurship-triple-bottom-brewing-company

Morrison, J. (2017, September 7). Are craft breweries the next coffeehouses? *The Smithsonian Magazine*. www.smithsonianmag.com/arts-culture/are-craft-breweries-next-coffeehouses-180964739/

Nave, E., Duarte, P., Rodrigues, R. G., Paço, A., Alves, H., & Oliveira, T. (2022). Craft beer – a systematic literature review and research agenda. *International Journal of Wine Business Research, 34*(2), 278–307. https://doi.org/10.1108/ ijwbr-05-2021-0029

New Zealand Health Promotion Agency. (2019). *Safer bars and restaurants: A guide to crime prevention through environmental design*.

Newell, A. (2012, June 13). Brewery vivant: The first LEED-certified microbrewery in the U.S. *TriplePundit*. www.triplepundit.com/story/2012/brewery-vivant-first-leed-certified-microbrewery-us/65431

Newman, K. (2022, August 25). How 5 drink pros are shining a light on native American culture. *Wine Enthusiast*. www.winemag.com/2022/08/25/how-5-drink-pros-are-shining-a-light-on-native-american-culture/

Niemi, L., & Kantola, J. (2018). Legitimated consumption: a socially embedded challenge for entrepreneurs' value creation. *Journal of Research in Marketing and Entrepreneurship*.

Nilsson, I., & Reid, N. (2019). The value of a craft brewery: On the relationship between craft breweries and property values. *Growth and Change, 50*(2), 689–704. https://doi.org/10.1111/grow.12292

Nilsson, I., Reid, N., & Lehnert, M. (2018). Geographic patterns of craft breweries at the intraurban scale. *The Professional Geographer, 70*(1), 114–125. https://doi.org/10.1080/00330124.2017.1338590

Nilsson, I., Smirnov, O., Reid, N., & Lehnert, M. (2019). To cluster or not to cluster? Spatial determinants of closures in the American craft brewing industry. *Papers in Regional Science, 98*(4), 1759–1778. https://doi.org/10.1111/pirs.12434

Nilsson, I., Wartell, J., & Reid, N. (2020). Craft breweries and neighborhood crime: Are they related? *Papers in Applied Geography, 6*(3), 256–271. https://doi.org/10.1080/23754931.2020.1737187

Noonan, G. A. (2017). A spatial analysis of the relationship between violent neighborhood crime rates and alternative gentrification indicators in Louisville, KY (2010–2016). *Electronic Theses and Dissertations.* Paper 2644. https://doi.org/10.18297/etd/2644

Nurin, T. (2018, March 5). Parents, don't let your babies grow up in breweries (or bars). *Forbes.* www.forbes.com/sites/taranurin/2018/03/05/parents-think-twice-before-bringing-your-babies-to-breweries-and-bars

O-20262 (SDMC). (2013). *Strikeout ordinance.* https://docs.sandiego.gov/council_reso_ordinance/rao2013/O-20262.pdf

O-20368 (SDMC). (2014). *Strikeout ordinance.* https://docs.sandiego.gov/municode_strikeout_ord/O-20368-SO.pdf

O-20481 (SDMC). (2015). https://docs.sandiego.gov/council_reso_ordinance/rao2015/O-20481.pdf

O-20752 (SDMC). (2017). *Strikeout ordinance.* https://docs.sandiego.gov/municode_strikeout_ord/O-20752-SO.pdf

OECD. (2019, April). Job polarization and work profile of the middle class. *COPE Policy Brief.* OECD Publishing, Paris, https://www.oecd.org/els/emp/Job-polarisation-and-the-work-profile-of-the-middle-class-Policy-brief-2019.pdf

Office of the City Clerk. (2023). *Municipal code.* City of San Diego. www.sandiego.gov/city-clerk/officialdocs/municipal-code

Ohio City. (2022). *Neighborhood guide.* www.ohiocity.org/guide#232

Olajire, A. A. (2020). The brewing industry and environmental challenges. *Journal of Cleaner Production, 256,* 102817. https://doi.org/10.1016/j.jclepro.2012.03.003

Oldenburg, R. (1989). *The great good place.* De Capo Press.

Oldenburg, R., & Brissett, D. (1982). The third place. *Qualitative Sociology, 5,* 265–284. https://doi.org/10.1007/BF00986754

Oregon Brewery Running Series. (2017, June 2). *Creating third spaces: Interview with colin rath, migration brewing* [Video]. YouTube. www.youtube.com/watch?v=eX0xDIvYVW0&feature=youtu.be

Patel, K., & Tierney, L. (2022, June 16). These maps illustrate the seriousness of the western drought. *The Washington Post.* www.washingtonpost.com/climate-environment/2022/06/16/drought-west-california-mountains/

Patterson, M. W., Hoalst-Pullen, N., & Chu, W. S. (2022). 10 Miles from a brewery: Population demographics and beer consumption patterns in the United States. *The Geographical Bulletin, 63*(1), 31–38.

Paul, D. J. (2017, October 17). 2017 Oregon brewers festival economic study and shortened 2018 festival. *Brewpublic.* https://brewpublic.com/beer-news/2017-oregon-brewers-festival-economic-study-shortened-2018-festival/

PDX (Portland) Dads Group. (2022). *Meetup.* www.meetup.com/PDXDadsGroup/

Petro, G. (2022, February 21). Gen Z and sustainability: The disruption has only just begun. *Forbes*. www.forbes.com/sites/gregpetro/2022/02/18/gen-z-and-sustainability-the-disruption-has-only-just-begun/?sh=2dcb2523eb74

Plastic Bank. (2022, December 15). *Impact programs – plastic bank*. https://plasticbank.com/impact-programs/

Plevoets, B., & Van Cleempoel, K. (2011). Adaptive reuse as a strategy towards conservation of cultural heritage: A literature review. In *Structural studies, repairs and maintenance of heritage architecture XII*. WIT Press.

Plummer, R., Telfer, D., & Hashimoto, A. (2008). The rise and fall of the waterloo-wellington ale trail: A study of collaboration within the tourism industry. *Current Issues in Tourism, 9*(3), 191–205. https://doi.org/10.2167/cit/194.0

Plummer, R., Telfer, D., Hashimoto, A., & Summers, R. J. (2005). Beer tourism in Canada, along the Waterloo-wellington ale trail. *Tourism Management, 26*(3), 447–458. https://doi.org/10.1016/j.tourman.2003.12.002

Pokrivčák, Jan & Chovanova Supekova, Sona & Lančarič, Drahoslav & Savov, Radovan & Tóth, Marián & Vašina, Radoslav. (2019). Development of beer industry and craft beer expansion. *Journal of Food and Nutrition Research, 58*, 63–74.

Porter, M. (1998, November–December). Clusters and the new economics of competition. *Harvard Business Review*. https://hbr.org/1998/11/clusters-and-the-new-economics-of-competition

Pridemore, W. A., & Grubesic, T. H. (2012). The effect of alcohol outlet density on violence. *The British Journal of Sociology, 63*, 680–703. https://doi.org/10.1111/j.1468-4446.2012.01432.x

Prison Break Brewery Apprenticeships. (2022). *Prison break brewery & OBN second chance initiative . . . providing second chances to those with a criminal past!* Prison Break Brewery. www.prisonbreakbrewery.com/apprenticeship

PubQuest. (2022). *Find a brewery*. https://pubquest.com/

Pullman, M. E., Greene, J., Liebmann, D., Ho, N., & Pedisich, X. (2015). Hopworks urban brewery: A case of sustainable beer. *PDXScholar, 30*. http://archives.pdx.edu/ds/psu/15644

Purcell, M., & Brown, J. C. (2005). Against the local trap: Scale and the study of environment and development. *Progress in Development Studies, 5*(4), 279–297. https://doi.org/10.1191/1464993405ps122oa

Pure Project. (2022, May 7). *The story of pure project*. www.purebrewing.org/story/

Quigley, B. M., K. E. Leonard, and R. L. Collins. (2003). Characteristics of violent bars and bar patrons. *Journal of Studies on Alcohol, 64*(6), 765–772. doi: 10.15288/jsa.2003.64.765.

Reid, N. (2018). Craft breweries, adaptive reuse, and neighborhood revitalization. *Urban Development Issues, 57*(1), 5–14. https://doi.org/10.2478/udi-2018-0013

Reid, N. (2020). Do craft breweries gentrify neighborhoods? It's complicated. *Salon*. www.salon.com/2020/01/13/are-craft-breweries-a-harbinger-of-gentrification-its-complicated/

Reid, N. (2021). Craft beer tourism: The search for authenticity, diversity, and great beer. *Regional Science Perspectives on Tourism and Hospitality, 1*, 317–337. https://doi.org/10.1007/978-3-030-61274-0_16

Reid, N., & Gatrell, J. D. (2015). Brewing growth. *Economic Development Journal, 14*(4), 5.

Reid, N, Gatrell, J. D., & Lehnert, M. (2020). Leveraging brewing history: The case of Cincinnati's over-the-Rhine neighborhood. In R. Thakur, A. K. Dutt, S. K. Thakur, & G. Pomeroy (Eds.), *Urban and regional planning and development: 20th Century forms and 21st century transformations.* Springer.

Reid, N., Gripshover, M. M., & Bell, T. L. (2019). Craft breweries and adaptive reuse in the USA: The use and reuse of space and language. In S. Brunn & R. Kehrein (Eds.), *Handbook of the changing world language map.* Springer.

Reid, N., & Nilsson, I. (2023). From mill district to brewery district: Craft beer and the revitalization of charlotte's NoDa neighborhood. In D. C. Harvey, E. Jones, & N. Chapman (Eds.), *Beer places: The micro-geographies of craft beer.* University of Arkansas Press.

Revington, N. (2018). Pathways and processes: Reviewing the role of young adults in urban structure. *The Professional Geographer, 70*(1), 1–10.

Rhode Island Department of Environmental Management. (2019, June 11). *IPP fact sheet – breweries, distilleries and wineries.* www.dem.ri.gov/programs/benviron/water/permits/ripdes/pdfs/brewery-ipp-fs.pdf

Rieger, S. (2021, July 6). This craft brewery is using carbon capture to reuse co2 in its brews. *CBC News.* www.cbc.ca/news/canada/calgary/blindman-brewing-carbon-capture-1.6091241

Robinson, M. (2019, January 24). *Stone brewing to invest $1M into facility expansion – stone brewing planning to invest $1 million into expansion of Fulton facility.* Richmond Times-Dispatch.

Roncek, D. W., & Maier, P. A. (1991). Bars, blocks, and crimes revisited: Linking the theory of routine activities to the empiricism of "hot spots". *Criminology, 29,* 725–753. http://dx.doi.org/10.1111/j.1745-9125.1991.tb01086.x

Rose, D. (1984). Home Ownership, Uneven Development and Industrial Change: The Making of a 'Separate Sphere' in Late Nineteenth Century Britain D Phil thesis, *Graduate Division of Geography,* University of Sussex, Falmer, Brighton BN1 9QN, England.

Rothstein, R. (2018). *The color of law: A forgotten history of how our government segregated America.* Liveright Publishing Corporation.

Rowe, P. (2010, May 18). *American craft beer week, May 17–23.* San Diego Union Tribune.

Rowe, P. (2013). *Liberty station's stone age begins.* The San Diego Union-Tribune.

Ryder, J. (2022, January 2). California expands successful apprenticeship program. *WorkingNation.* workingnation.com/california-expands-successful-apprenticeship-program

Salovaara, P. (2021). "Come One, Come All? The Impact of Craft Breweries on Revitalisation and Community-Building", Clarke, D., Ellis, V., Patrick-Thomson, H. and Weir, D. (Eds.) *Researching Craft Beer: Understanding Production, Community and Culture in An Evolving Sector,* Emerald Publishing Limited, Bingley, pp. 175–193. https://doi.org/10.1108/978-1-80043-184-320211012

San Diego Brewers Guild. (2023). *Welcome to the capital of craft beer.* www.sdbeer.com

San Diego State University Global Campus. (2022, December 29). *Professional certificate in the business of craft beer.* San Diego State University. https://ces.sdsu.edu/hospitality/professional-certificate-business-craft-beer

Schmidt, C., Cornelisse, S., Crissy, H., & Devlin, K. (2021). *Craft beverage trail collaborations in Pennsylvania: A resource for breweries and destination marketing organizations*. NERCRD. bit.ly/PA-beer-trails

Schnell, S. M., & Reese, J. F. (2014). Microbreweries, place, and identity in the United States. In N. Hoalst-Pullen & M. Patterson (Eds.), *The geography of beer*. Springer.

Schroeder, S. K. (2020). Crafting new lifestyles and urban places: The craft beer scene of Berlin. *Papers in Applied Geography, 6*(3), 204–221. https://doi.org/10.1080/23 754931.2020.1776149

Scott, J. (2013, January 16). Alaskan brewing adds another energy saving tool. *Realbeer*. www.realbeer.com/alaskan-brewing-adds-another-energy-saving-tool/

Scott, M., & Dedel, K. (2006). *Assaults in and around bars* (2nd ed.). Arizona State University.

Sherman, L. W., Schmidt, J. D., & Velke, R. J. (1992). *High crime taverns: A RECAP (repeat call address policing) project in problem-oriented policing*. U.S. Department of Justice.

Shin, R., & Searcy, C. (2018). Evaluating the greenhouse gas emissions in the craft beer industry: An assessment of challenges and benefits of greenhouse gas accounting. *Sustainability, 10*, 4191. https://doi.org/10.3390/su10114191

Shortridge, J. R. (1996). Keeping Tabs on Kansas: Reflections on Regionally Based Field Study. *Journal of Cultural Geography, 16*(1), 5–16.

Singh, R. K., Murty, H. R., Gupta, S. K., & Dikshit, A. K. (2009). An overview of sustainability assessment methodologies. *Indicators, 9*(2), 189–212.

Sisson, P. (2017, June 13). Craft beer's big impact on small towns and forgotten neighborhoods. *Curbed*. https://archive.curbed.com/2017/6/13/15788960/brewing-economic-development-craft-beer

Sjölander-Lindqvist, A., Skoglund, W., & Laven, D. (2019). Craft beer – building social terroir through connecting people, place and business. *Journal of Place Management and Development, 13*(2), 149–162. https://doi.org/10.1108/JPMD-01-2019-0001

Skypeck, C. (2020). Beer's critical ingredient: Water. *The New Brewer: The Journal of the Brewers Association, 37*(1), 43–44.

Slaper, T. F., & Hall, T. J. (2011). *The triple bottom line: What is it and how does it work?* Indiana Business Review.

Smith, G. S., Breakstone, H., Dean, L. T., & Thorpe Jr., R. J. (2020). Impacts of gentrification on health in the US: A systematic review of the literature. *Journal of Urban Health, 97*, 845–856. https://doi.org/10.1007/s11524-020-00448-4

Smith, K. (2018, October 12). How many craft breweries are too many? Anaheim's got 15 and more are on the way. *The Orange County Register*. www.ocregister.com/2018/10/11/how-many-craft-breweries-are-too-many-anaheims-got-15-and-more-are-on-the-way/

Smith, N. & Williams, P. (1986). *Gentrification of the City*. United Kingdom: Allen & Unwin.

Smith, N. (2006). Gentrification generalized: From local anomaly to urban 'regeneration' as global urban strategy. In G. Downey & M. Fisher (Eds.), *Frontiers of capital: Ethnographic reflections on the new economy*. Duke University Press.

Somerville, H. (2013, July 16). Oakland: Craft beer trend helps rebuild neighborhoods. *San Jose Mercury-News*. www.mercurynews.com/2013/07/16/oakland-craft-beer-trend-helps-rebuild-neighborhoods/

Sonoma County Economic Development Board. (2013). *Sonoma county craft beverage report 2013*. Sonoma County Economic Development Board.

Sonoma County Economic Development Board. (2022). *Russian River Brewing Co. Pliny the Younger release 2022 economic impact*. Sonoma County Economic Development Board.

State of New York, Office of Planning and Development. (2021). *From rust-belt to beer-belt: Craft beer and downtown revitalization in upstate New York*. www.ny.gov/sites/default/files/atoms/files/DRI_CaseStudy_CraftBeer.pdf

Stocker, F., Abib, G., Jhunior, R. D. O. S., & Irigaray, H. A. R. (2021). Brazilian craft breweries and internationalization in the born global perspective. *Revista de Gestão*, *28*(2), 163–178. https://doi.org/10.1108/REGE-01-2021-0014

Stocks, C., Barker, A. J., & Guy, S. (2012). The composting of brewery sludge. *Journal of the Institute of Brewing*, *108*(4), 452–458. https://doi.org/10.1002/j.2050-0416.2002.tb00575.x

Stoilova, E. (2020). Craft beer culture and creative industries in Plovdiv, Bulgaria. *Papers in Applied Geography*, *6*(3), 222–239.

Stone Brewing. (2012, January 11). *Stone brewing co. Greg Koch talks at google* [Video]. Youtube. www.youtube.com/watch?v=JWod0jxZnTo

Stone Brewing. (2014, October 9). *Stone brewing co. – Richmond, VA* [Video]. Youtube. www.youtube.com/watch?v=pq5bLK_wCRo

Stone Brewing. (2015, April 10). *Stonelandia: Myths of stone, Pt. 3* [Video]. YouTube. www.youtube.com/watch?v=V3HElZVcOM0&t=364s

Stone Brewing. (2016, April 30). *e.g. 2016 – Greg Koch* [Video]. YouTube. www.youtube.com/watch?v=Ow8oWdh90Vg&t=690s

Stone Brewing. (2023, November 22). *Our story*. Stone Brewing. www.stonebrewing.com/about/history

Stone, M. J., Garibaldi, R., & Pozzi, A. (2020). Motivation, behaviors, and travel activities of beer tourists. *Tourism Review International*, *24*(2–3), 167–178. https://doi.org/10.3727/154427220X15912253254437

Strohacker, K., Fitzhugh, E. C., Wozencroft, A., Ferrara, P. M. M., & Beaumont, C. T. (2021). Promotion of leisure-time physical activity by craft breweries in Knoxville, Tennessee. *Leisure Studies*, *40*(6), 854–871. https://doi.org/10.1080/02614367.2021.1933574

Sweetwood, M. (Director). (2019). *Beer Jesus from America*. [Film]. Sweetwood Films.

Sutton, S. A. (2010). Rethinking Commercial Revitalization: A Neighborhood Small Business Perspective. *Economic Development Quarterly*, *24*(4), 352–371. https://doi.org/10.1177/0891242410370679

Talmage, C. A., Denicourt, J. C., Delpha, P. J., Goodwin, G. B., & Snyder, E. B. (2020). Exploring neolocalism among finger lakes breweries and local communities: Merits and cautions. *Local Development & Society*, *1*(2), 140–159. https://doi.org/10.1080/26883597.2020.1801332

Tengö, M., & Andersson, E. (2002). Solutions-oriented research for sustainability: Turning knowledge into action. *Ambio*, *51*, 25–30. https://doi.org/10.1007/s13280-020-01492-9

Thomas, K. R., & Rahman, P. (2006). Brewery wastes. Strategies for sustainability. A review. *Aspects of Applied Biology*, *80*, 147–153.

Thornhill, J. (2020, June 26). Craft beer brewer feeds CO2 emissions to tanks of hungry algae. *Bloomberg*. www.bloomberg.com/news/articles/2020-06-26/craft-beer-brewer-feeds-co2-emissions-to-tanks-of-hungry-algae

Tokos, H., Pintaric, Z. N., & Krajnc, D. (2012). An integrated sustainability performance assessment and benchmarking of breweries. *Clean Technologies and Environmental Policy, 14*(2), 173–193. https://doi.org/10.1007/s10098-011-0390-0

Toomey, T. L., Erickson, D. J., Carlin, B. P., Lenk, K. M., Quick, H. S., Jones, A. M. & Harwood. E. M. (2012). The association between density of alcohol establishments and violent crime within urban neighborhoods. *Alcoholism: Clinical and Experimental Research, 36*(8), 1468–1473. doi: 10.1111/j.1530-0277.2012.01753.x

Toth, G. (2020). *Beyond metrics: Breweries aim for B Corp certification*. The New Brewer. Brewers Association.

Tremblay, V. J., Iwasaki, N., & Tremblay, C. H. (2005). The dynamics of industry concentration for U.S. Micro and macro brewers. *Review of Industrial Organization, 26*(3), 307–324. https://doi.org/10.1007/s11151-004-8114-9

Tremblay, V. J., Tremblay, V. J., & Tremblay, C. H. (2005). *The US brewing industry: Data and economic analysis*. MIT Press.

Triple Bottom Brewing. (n.d.). *Mission*. https://triplebottombrewing.com/mission

Twinam, T. (2017). Danger zone: Land use and the geography of neighborhood crime. *Journal of Urban Economics, 100*, 104–119. https://doi.org/10.1016/j.jue.2017.05.006

United States Bureau of Labor Statistics. (2018). *QCEW data views*. data.bls.gov/cew/apps/data_views/data_views.htm#tab=Tables

United States Bureau of Labor Statistics. (2022, November). *Employment and earnings table B-1A*. www.bls.gov/web/empsit/ceseeb1a.htm

United States Census Bureau. (1995, August). *County business patterns: 1993*. www.census.gov/data/datasets/1993/econ/cbp/1993-cpb.html

United States Census Bureau. (2021). *Educational attainment. 1-year estimate, 2021 American community survey*. https://data.census.gov/table?q=Educational+Attainment&tid=ACSST1Y2021.S1501

United States Census Bureau. (2022). *County Business Patterns: 2020*. www.census.gov/data/datasets/2020/econ/cbp/2020-cbp.html

University of California (UC) San Diego Division of Extended Studies. (2022). *About the brewing program*. UC San Diego. https://extendedstudies.ucsd.edu/courses-and-programs/brewing

University of California Television. (2013, May 16). *Good beer, good food and good business with stone brewing's Greg Koch* [Video]. YouTube. www.youtube.com/watch?v=n_jpnjM4P78&t=254s

Vicario, L., & Martinez Monje, P. M. (2003). Another "Guggenheim effect"? The generation of a potentially gentrifiable neighbourhood in Bilbao. *Urban Studies, 40*(12), 2383–2400. https://doi.org/10.1080/0042098032000136129

Villanueva, M. (2014, December). *Creating a strategic plan for local economic development: A guide. Federation of Canadian municipalities – Caribbean local economic development project*. Organization of American States. www.oas.org/en/sedi/dsd/

VisitCalgary.com. (2022, May 11). *Calgary's brewery districts*. www.visitcalgary.com/things-to-do/stories-from-calgary/tour-calgarys-brewery-districts

Walker, S., & Fox Miller, C. (2018). Have craft breweries followed or led gentrification in Portland, Oregon? An investigation of retail and neighbourhood change. *Geografiska Annaler: Series B, Human Geography, 101*(2), 102–117. https://doi.org/10.1080/04353684.2018.1504223

Walks, R. A., & Maaranen, R. (2008). Gentrification, social mix, and social polarization: Testing the linkages in large Canadian cities. *Urban Geography, 29*(4), 293–326. https://doi.org/10.2747/0272-3638.29.4.293

Wallace, A. (2019). "Brewing the truth": Craft beer, class and place in contemporary London. *Sociology, 53*(5). https://doi.org/10.1177/0038038519833913

Ward, C. (2016, December 12). Lawrenceville, a history of change. *Steel City Renaissance.* www.pointclickpgh.com/F16/?p=319

Wartell, J. (2016). *Analysis of bars, breweries and police calls for service in Portland, OR.* Unpublished.

Wartell, J. (2017). *Analysis of last drink surveys in Ventura County, CA.* Unpublished.

Watne, T. A., & Hakala, H. (2013). Inventor, founder or developer? An enquiry into the passion that drives craft breweries in Victoria, Australia. *Journal of Marketing Development and Competitiveness, 7*(3), 54–67.

Watson, B. (2018, December 10). Brewery growth is both urban and rural. *Brewers Association.* www.brewersassociation.org/insights/brewery-growth-both-urban-and-rural/

Watson, B. (2020). Leaders and laggards in U.S. Brewing: Political trajectories and brewery density. In N. Hoalst-Pullen & M. Patterson (Eds.), *The geography of beer.* Springer.

Watson, B. (2020, June 25). The geography and demographics of small brewers, part 1. *Brewers Association.* www.brewersassociation.org/insights/the-geography-and-demographics-of-small-brewers-part-1/

Watson, B. (2021, October 5). New owner demographic benchmarking data. *Brewers Association.* www.brewersassociation.org/insights/new-owner-demographic-benchmarking-data/

Watson, B. (2022, September 8). Economic impact, economic impact. *Brewers Association.* www.brewersassociation.org/statistics-and-data/economic-impact-data/

Weiler, S. (2000). Pioneers and settlers in Lo-Do Denver: Private risk and public benefits in urban redevelopment. *Urban Studies, 37*(1), 167–179. https://doi.org/10.1080/0042098002348

Weirsch, A. M., Misera, L., Marre, A., & Wavering Corcoran, E. (2021). *Small business credit survey, 2022 report on employer firms.* United States Federal Reserve System.

Wells, J. (2014, August). Brewery vivant becomes the newest B Corp-certified brewery. *BeerAdvocate.* www.beeradvocate.com/articles/11506/brewery-vivant-becomes-the-newest-b-corp-certified-brewery/

West Virginia Department of Commerce. (2020, November 10). Apprenticeships – brewing up a new talent pipeline to the second fastest growing manufacturing industry in WV, the craft beer industry. *Westvirginia.gov.* https://westvirginia.gov/apprenticeships-brewing-up-a-new-talent-pipeline-to-the-second-fastest-growing-manufacturing-industry-in-wv-the-craft-beer-industry/

Whyte, M. (2020, January 14). 'My Parkdale is gone': How gentrification reached the one place that seemed immune. *The Guardian.* www.theguardian.com/cities/2020/jan/14/my-parkdale-is-gone-how-gentrification-reached-the-one-place-that-seemed-immune

Williams, A. (2017). Exploring the impact of legislation on the development of craft beer. *Beverages, 3*(4), 18. https://doi.org/10.3390/beverages3020018

Wojtyra, B. (2020). How and why did craft breweries 'revolutionise' the beer market? The case of Poland. *Moravian Geographical Reports, 28*(2), 81–97. https://doi.org/10.2478/mgr-2020-0007

Woodard, C. (2016, June 16). How Cincinnati salvaged the nation's most dangerous neighborhood. *Politico Magazine.* www.politico.com/magazine/story/2016/06/what-works-cincinnati-ohio-over-the-rhine-crimeneighborhood-turnaround-city-urban-revitalization-213969

Yee, V. (2015, November 27). Gentrification in a Brooklyn Neighborhood Forces Residents to Move On. The New York Times. Available from: https://www.nytimes.com/2015/11/29/nyregion/gentrification-in-a-brooklyn-neighborhood-forces-residents-to-move-on.html [accessed: 03.05.2018]. Yee, 27.

Zaniewski, A. (2014). Bar's 'No colors' sign raises uproar on social media. *USA Today.* www.usatoday.com/story/news/nation/2014/02/06/bar-sign-no-colors-facebook-uproar/5252545/

Zuk, M., Bierbaum, A. H., Chapple, K., Gorska, K., & Loukaitou-Sideris, A. (2018). Gentrification, displacement, and the role of public investment. *Journal of Planning Literature, 33*(1), 31–44. https://doi.org/10.1177/0885412217716439

Index

For Product Safety Concerns and Information please contact our EU
representative GPSR@taylorandfrancis.com
Taylor & Francis Verlag GmbH, Kaufingerstraße 24, 80331 München, Germany